CW00740730

Published by Cypress Hills Press
Brooklyn, New York

Book design: Richard Tackett
http://www.richtackett.com

THE CARRY ON FILMS

BY

SCOTT PALMER

INTRODUCTION

This is a reference book about the *Carry On* films, which were made between 1957 and 1992. The book includes all the films in date order, complete cast listings, numerous photographs, directorial credits, running times, and a story synopsis for each film.

The *Carry On* series of 32 British comedy films was released between 1957 and 1992, directed by Gerald Thomas and produced by Peter Rogers. *Carry On Admiral*, made in 1957, was the only film not done by Rogers and Thomas, although it was a comedy and featured several of the series regulars, notably Joan Sims and Joan Hickson.

The humour of the films was bawdy and reminiscent of the music hall days. The stock-in-trade of *Carry On* humour was innuendo (the Italian word for Preparation H) and the sending-up of British institutions and customs.

31 of the films were produced by Peter Rogers and directed by Gerald Thomas. They also did a 1975 TV series, as well as four Christmas specials between 1969 and 1973, as well as plays in the West End.

The *Carry On* series contains the greatest number of films of any British series, and it is the second-longest running British film series, after the James Bond films.

All the films were made at Pinewood Studios; Amglo Amalgamated Film Distributors Ltd. produced twelve films (1958–1966), and The Rank Organization made eighteen (1966–1978).

The films adhered to a strict budget, and often employed the same crew; budgetary constraints meant that a large proportion of the location filming was undertaken close to the studios in and around south Buckinghamshire.

Later films in the series used locations in Wales and the beaches of the Sussex coast. The films often followed a theme in which a small group of misfit newcomers to a job make comic mistakes, but come together to succeed in the end.

The actors were not well paid-around £5,000 per film for the leads. Producer Peter Rogers once remarked that while the stars cost very little to employ, they made money for the franchise. The audiences liked the films a lot more than the critics.

Regular performers in the series included Sidney James, Hattie Jacques, Kenneth Williams, Charles Hawtrey, Kenneth Connor, Joan Sims, Peter Butterworth, Barbara Windsor, Terry Scott, and Bernard Bresslaw.

TABLE OF CONTENTS

CARRY ON ADMIRAL (1957)

DIRECTED BY Val Guest

CAST

David Tomlinson.....................Tom Baker
Peggy Cummins.............Susan Lashwood
Brian Reece............................Peter Fraser
A.E. Matthews...............Admiral Godfrey
Eunice Gayson....................Jane Godfrey
Joan Sims...Mary
Lionel Murton........................Psychiatrist
Reginald Beckwith................Receptionist
Desmond Walter-Ellis...Willy Oughton-Formby
Ronald Shiner.....................Salty Simpson
Peter Coke...........................Lt. Lashwood
Derek Blomfield.....................Lr. Dobson
Tom Gill...............................Petty Officer
Howard Williams..............Sub-Lieutenant
Joan Hickson...................................Mother
John Timberlake.............................Father
Toke Townley.............................Steward
Ronald Adam.....................First Sea Lord
Sam Kydd................................Attendant
Philip Ashley.........................First Officer
Harold Goodwin............................Parker
Everley Gregg.......................Housekeeper
David Hannaford................................Alfie
Victor Harrington................Naval Officer
James Hayter...........Sir Henry Tomkinson
Walter Horsbrugh........Night Receptionist
Emrys Leyshon.................Radio Operator

David Tomlinson Peggy Cummins Brian Reece

A.E. Matthews Eunice Gayson Joan Sims

Lionel Murton Reginald Beckwith Desmond Walter-Ellis

Ronald Shiner Peter Coke Derek Blomfield

Tom Gill Howard Williams Joan Hickson

George Moon.....................................Casey
Donald Pickering...............Second Officer
Jimmy Ray...Bert
James Sharkey...................Dispatch Rider
Alfie Bass, Arthur Lovegrove.....Orderlies
Richard Duke, Roy Everson......Crewmen

John Timberlake   Toke Townley   Ronald Adam

Sam Kydd   Harold Goodwin   Everley Gregg

David Hannaford   Victor Harrington   James Hayter   Walter Horsbrugh   George Moon   Alfie Bass   Arthur Lovegrove

Richard Duke   Roy Everson   Hotel Porter   Sailor 1   Sailor 2   Steward

83 minutes

In the course of a drunken reunion, two old friends change places (one a junior government minister, the other a Roayl Navy officer in uniform about to take command for the first time),

They switch clothes before passing out. Next morning, their changed clothes result in a series of cases of mistaken identity. The film follows the efforts of each to reunite himself with his own destiny.

Peggy Cummins, Ronald Shiner

8

The former's lack of sea knowledge causes several catastrophes, including torpedoing the First Lord of The Admiralty.

Captain Peter Fraser is in town as he is due to take command of the HMS Sherwood in the morning but he finds himself bumping into an old friend, Tom Baker, who is a secretary for the Admiralty.

As they decide to have a drink, one leads to another and another before they are not only drunk but have swapped clothes and rooms.

Come the next day Tom is mistaken for Peter and before he knows it finds himself aboard the battleship whilst Peter finds himself having to do Tom's job.

David Tomlinson, Peggy Cummins, Sam Kydd

PeterCoke, David Tomlinson, Derek Blomfield

Foreign Film Poster

U.S. Lobby Card

A.E. Matthews, Brian Reece

Baker is awakened by some of Fraser's officers, who have never met him and mistake Baker for their new captain. With both men stuck in their new roles, they try to keep afloat long enough to swap places again.

One reviewer stated "Although not too well known, the film is interesting inasmuch as nearly all the supporting and uncredited roles are played by well-known actors. Familiar faces like Joan Sims, Joan Hickson, Alfie Bass, and the ubiquitous Sam Kydd, all made the film worth watching. It almost ran like a potted history of British Cinema of the 1950s and '60s."

Film Poster

A.E. Matthews with portrait

David Tomlinson, A.E. Matthews

Another said "Although it has only an average plot the 1957 film of an Ian Hay stage play is worth seeing for three reasons. First, it has some great cameos by a range of British bit-part actors, including a perplexed Reginald Beckwith, a young Joan Sims, a lugubrious Ronald Shiner, a too-short appearance by Alfie Bass and uncredited James Hayter.

A.E. Matthews, Eunice Gayson

Lobby Card

Lobby Card

Foreign Film Poster

Joan Sims, Brian Reece, David Tomlinson

Secondly, it has a barnstorming appearance by the elderly British character actor A.E. Matthews who was in his late 80s when the film was shot and had been playing the same role of a peppery old admiral/colonel etc for decades. He fluffs a few lines but carries the film along with his enthusiasm. Finally David Tomlinson, one of Britain's finest comedy actors, is a joy to behold. His comic timing is faultless and he lights up every scene he's in."

Film Poster

U.S. Lobby Card

Eunice Gayson, A.E. Matthews, James Hayter

Eunice Gayson, Peggy Cummins, A.E. Matthews

A.E. Matthews, Desmond Walter-Ellis

Lobby Card

12

CARRY ON SERGEANT (1958)

DIRECTED BY GERALD THOMAS

CAST

William Hartnell.......Sergeant Grimshawe
Shirley Eaton.............................Mary Sage
Bob Monkhouse....................Charlie Sage
Eric Barker............................Captain Potts
Dora Bryan..Norah
Bill Owen....................Corporal Copping
Kenneth Williams.................James Bailey
Charles Hawtrey................Peter Golightly
Kenneth Connor.................Horace Strong
Terence Longdon.............Miles Heywood
Norman Rossington...........Herbert Brown
Gerald Campion...............Andy Calloway
Hattie Jacques.....................Captain Clark
Cyril Chamberlain...............Gun Sergeant
Anthony Sagar..................Stores Sergeant
Ian Whittaker.................Medical Corporal
Ed Devereaux.................Sergeant Russell
Terry Scott.....................Sergeant O'Brien
Martin Wyldeck..........................Mr. Sage
Helen Goss...............................Mrs. Sage
Leigh Madison.............................Sheila
Bernard Foreman..............Lance Corporal
Joe Phelps....................................Corporal
John Mathews, Jimmy Millar.....Sergeants
Ken Hutchins, Reg Thomason.....Soldiers
Martin Boddey, Arnold Diamond, Basil Dignam, Frank Forsyth, John Gatrell,

William Hartnell

Shirley Eaton

Bob Monkhouse

Eric Barker

Dora Bryan

Bill Owen

Kenneth Williams

Charles Hawtrey

Kenneth Connor

Terence Longdon

Norman Rossington

Gerald Campion

Hattie Jacques

Cyril Chamberlain

Anthony Sagar

Gordon Tanner..........................Specialists
Alec Bregonzi, Ronald Clarke, Pat Fee-
ney, Alexander Harris, Edward Judd, Gra-
ham Stewart, David Williams....Storemen
Hyma Beckley, Ernest Blythe, Muriel
Greenslade, Vic Hagan, Billy John, Gerry
Judge, Bunny Seaman, John Tatum...........
....Wedding Guests
Rodney Cardiff, Ivor Danvers, Jeremy
Dempster, Terry Dickinson, Nicholas
Donnelly, Patrick Durkin, Leon Eagles,
Graydon Gould, Earl Green, Norman
Hartley, Michael Hunt, Brian Jackson,
Bernard Kay, Benny Lee, Ken Lewing-
ton, Henry Livings, Don McCorkindale,
Derek Martinus, Arnold Schulkes, Jack
Smethurst, James Villiers, Haydn Ward,
Malcolm Webster, Bob Wright..................
....New Recruits

Ian Whittaker

Ed Devereaux

Terry Scott

Martin Wyldeck

Helen Goss

Leigh Madison

Bernard Foreman

Joe Phelps

John Mathews

Jimmy Millar

Ken Hutchins

Reg Thomason

Martin Boddey   Arnold Diamond

Basil Dignam

Frank Forsyth

John Gatrell   Gordon Tanner

Alec Bregonzi

Ronald Clarke

Pat Feeney

Alexander Harris

Edward Judd

Graham Stewart

David Williams

Hyma Beckley

Ernest Blythe

Muriel Greenslade

Vic Hagan

Billy John

Gerry Judge

Bunny Seaman

John Tatum

Rodney Cardiff | Jeremy Dempster | Terry Dickinson | Nicholas Donnelly | Patrick Durkin | Leon Eagles | Graydon Gould

Earl Green | Michael Hunt | Brian Jackson | Bernard Kay | Ken Lewington | Henry Livings | Don McCorkindale

Derek Martinus | Arnold Schulkes | Jack Smethurst | James Villiers | Haydn Ward | Malcolm Webster | Bob Wright

Soldier 1 | Soldier 2 | Soldier 3 | Soldier 4 | Woman | New Recruit

84 minutes

Newly married Mary Sage is distraught when her husband Charlie receives his call-up papers during their wedding breakfast. He has no choice but to report.

He travels to Heathercrest National Service Depot, meeting fellow recruit Horace Strong, a chronic hypochondriac who is devastated at having been passed as fit.

Hattie Jacques, Kenneth Connor

William Hartnell as Sergeant Grimshawe

15

The new recruits are assigned to Sergeant Grimshawe. Grimshawe will soon be retiring from the army and takes on a £50 bet with Sergeant O'Brien that his last bunch of men will be his first champion platoon.

With beady-eyed inspection from Captain Potts and disgruntled support from Corporal Copping, Grimshawe decides to use some psychology and treat his charges kindly rather than simply shouting at them. But basic training does not start well and he struggles to take his platoon through it. They include failure Herbert Brown, upper-class cad Miles Heywood, rock 'n' roller Andy Galloway, delicate flower Peter Golightly, and supercilious university graduate James Bailey. His attempts seem doomed.

Foreign Film Poster

Film Poster

Bob Monkhouse, Shirley Eaton

Group in the barracks

William Hartnell, Charles Hawtrey

Mary is determined to spend her wedding night with her husband and smuggles herself into the depot to get a job in the NAAFI, a situation Charlie is eventually able to legitimize.

Strong spends most of his time complaining to the Medical Officer, Captain Clark. It is only the adoration of doe-eyed NAAFI girl Norah, which he initially rejects, that makes him realize his potential and inspires him to become a real soldier.

Film Poster

Bob and Shirley have a pint

Kenneth Williams, Norman Rossington, Gerald Campion, Bob Monkhouse. Terence Longdon, Charles Hawtrey

Kenneth Williams, Eric Barker

Bob Monkhouse, Kenneth Connor

Bob Monkhouse & Shirley Eaton

17

Bob Monkhouse, Shirley Eaton,
Dora Bryan

Gerald Campion, Bob Monkhouse,
William Hartnell

Charles Hawtrey, Terence Longdon

Hattie Jacques, Kenneth Connor,
Gordon Tanner

Lobby Card

Movie Still

Film Poster

On the eve of the final tests, Grimshawe is in despair, but he is overheard bemoaning his lot to Copping. The squad decides to win the best platoon prize at all costs. On the day, they indeed beat the other platoons at all tasks and Grimshawe is awarded the cup for best platoon.

18

CARRY ON NURSE (1959)

Directed by Gerald Thomas

CAST

Shirley Eaton....................Dorothy Denton
Wilfrid Hyde-White...............The Colonel
Leslie Phillips.............................Jack Bell
Kenneth Connor.................Bernie Bishop
Charles Hawtrey...........Humphrey Hinton
Hattie Jacques................................Matron
Kenneth Williams...............Oliver Reckitt
Terence Longdon........................Ted York
Bill Owen...........................Percy Hickson
Joan Sims............................Stella Dawson
Susan Stephen..................Georgie Axwell
Susan Beaumont......Nurse Frances James
Ann Firbank............................Helen Lloyd
Joan Hickson......................................Sister
Cyril Chamberlain.......................Bert Able
Harry Locke..Mick
Norman Rossington............................Norm
Brian Oulton............................Henry Bray
Susan Shaw............................Jane Bishop
Jill Ireland.........................Jill Thompson
Irene Handl........................Madge Hickson
Michael Medwin.............................Ginger
Leigh Madison............................Dr. Winn
John Van Eyssen........................Stephens
Marianne Stone........................Alice Able
Rosalind Knight...........Nurse Nightingale
June Whitfield.....................................Meg

Shirley Eaton   Wilfrid Hyde-White   Leslie Phillips

Kenneth Connor   Charles Hawtrey   Hattie Jacques

Kenneth Williams   Terence Longdon   Bill Owen

Joan Sims   Susan Stephen   Susan Beaumont

Ann Firbank   Joan Hickson   Cyril Chamberlain

19

Hilda Fenemore......................Rhoda Bray
Frank Forsyth.........................John Gray
Ed Devereaux.....................Alec Lawrence
Martin Boddey..............................Perkins
Fred Griffiths...................Ambulance Man
John Matthews....................Tom Mayhew
Graham Stewart...................George Field
Marita Stanton.......................Rose Harper
Patrick Durkin............................Jackson
Anthony Sagar.................Ambulance Man
Shane Cordell..................Attractive Nurse
Christine Ozanne..........................Cleaner
Lucy Griffiths........................Trolley Lady
Charles Stanley..............................Porter
David Williams..............Andrew Newman
Jeremy Connor...................Jeremy Bishop
Stephanie Schiller....................New Nurse
Fred Machon..................................Doctor
Reg Thomason...............................Porter
Jack Dearlove...............................Patient
Raymond Glendenning..Racing Commentator

AND: Jack Armstrong, Alan Beaton, Tony
Castleton, Otto Friese, Alan Gibbs, Fred
Haggerty, Aidan Harrington, Dee Hart,
John Ketteringham, Marjorie Lyons, Ter-
ence Maidment, Rosalind Mendleson,
Tony Mendleson, Manny Michael, George
Miller, John Moyce, Peter Pocock, Pat
Ryan, Prunella Smith, Christine Spooner,
John Tatum, June West

Harry Locke Norman Rossington Brian Oulton

Susan Shaw Jill Ireland Irene Handl

Michael Medwin Leigh Madison John Van Eyssen

Marianne Stone Rosalind Knight June Whitfield

Hilda Fenemore Frank Forsyth Ed Devereaux

Martin Boddey Fred Griffiths Graham Stewart

Marita Stanton Patrick Durkin Anthony Sagar Shane Cordell Christine Ozanne Lucy Griffiths Charles Stanley

David Williams Jeremy Connor Fred Machon Reg Thomason Jack Dearlove Jack Armstrong Tony Castleton

Otto Friese Fred Haggerty Tony Mendleson Manny Michael Pat Ryan John Tatum

86 minutes

Irene Handl, Bill Owen

An ambulance arrives at top speed to Haven Hospital, carrying newsman Ted York, who has been struck with appendicitis. Ted is put to bed and is immediately smitten with the lovely Nurse Denton. The other nurses are constantly having to respond to the calls of the Colonel, who has a private room. He is an inveterate gambler and is having his bets placed by Mick, the orderly.

Terence Longdon, Martin Boddey

Later that day, Bernie Bishop, a prizefighter, is admitted after breaking his hand during a fight. Under the watchful eye of the Sister, patients and nurses alike are made ready for the Matron's inspection. Matron checks on the progress of the patients, and speaks to Mr. Hinton, who is forever listening to the radio with his headphones. Mick and the Colonel wager how long the Matron will take on her rounds.

Shirley Eaton, Joan Hickson

Joan Sims, Joan Hickson

21

Meanwhile Ted decides to write an article on his experiences as a hospital patient. He notices that Nurse Denton is quite fond of one of the doctors, but the man seems too busy to notice her. When Nurse Dawson, a clumsy probationer, rings the bell to signal the end of visiting hours, she mistakenly sets off the fire alarm.

The bookish intellectual Oliver Reckitt is visited by Jill, the sister of his friend Harry. They clearly like each other, but are too shy to admit it. Bernie, who has been told he will not be able to box for several months due to his hand injury, urges Oliver to admit how he really feels about Jill.

When Nurse Dawson comes in early to sterilize some rubber catheters, she is interrupted by the demanding Colonel. The catheters are put in a kidney dish to boil on the stove, but are forgotten about and catch on fire.

Wilfrid Hyde-White, Terence Longdon

Hattie Jacques, Joan Hickson

Joan Sims, Leslie Phillips

Harry Locke, Joan Sims

Film Poster

Wilfrid Hyde-White reading

Jack Bell arrives to have a bunion removed and is placed in the ward. Jill comes to see Oliver and they admit that they care for each other. She gives him a candy bar as a gift, but when he eats it, it makes him sick. Mr. Able complains that he can't sleep as he has been missing his wife. He is put on medication, but it makes him wildly excited and he runs amok in the hospital.

Bell's operation is delayed, which upsets him greatly as he is planning a romantic weekend. He offers the men in the ward the champagne he was going to drink with his girl-friend. They all get drunk and decide to remove the bunion them-selves. The night nurse is tied up and Hinton disguises himself as the nurse.

Harry Locke, Joan Sims

Kenneth Connor, Susan Shaw

Cyril Chamberlain & Kenneth Williams

Brian Oulton, Hilda Fenemore

Kenneth Williams, Jill Ireland

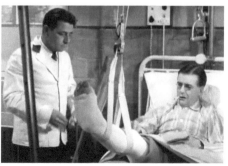

Harry Locke, Bill Owen

23

Jack begins to have second thoughts as Oliver begins the operation; laughing gas however has been turned on, leaks out, and everyone succumbs to fits of laughter. Fortunately a nurse arrives and sends everyone back to where they belong.

The Colonel attaches a piece of paper with a large scarlet letter on Nurse Dawson's back as a prank.. Ted discovers that Nurse Denton is applying for a job in America and tries to talk her out of it.

Jack catches a cold and his operation is postponed yet again. Oliver is discharged and leaves with Jill, and Bernie is met by his young son and they leave together. Ted is also discharged and makes a date with Nurse Denton. Nurse Dawson and Nurse Axwell decide to get even with the Colonel and replace a rectal thermometer with a daffodil.

Susan Stephen, Wilfrid Hyde-White

Wilfrid Hyde-White as the Colonel

Ann Firbank, Rosalind Knight

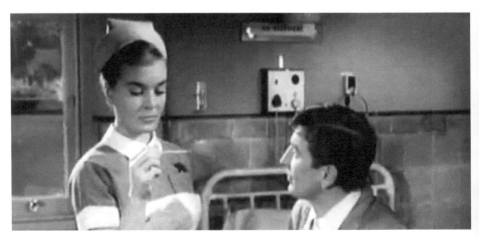

Shirley Eaton, Terence Longdon

CARRY ON TEACHER (1959)

DIRECTED BY Gerald Thomas

CAST

Ted Ray....Headmaster William Wakefield
Hattie Jacques........................Grace Short
Kenneth Williams...............Edwin Milton
Joan Sims...........................Sarah Alcock
Leslie Phillips...................Alistair Gregg
Rosalind Knight.............Felicity Wheeler
Kenneth Connor...............Gregory Adams
Charles Hawtrey.................Michael Bean
Richard O'Sullivan.............Robin Stevens
Carol White...........................Sheila Dale
Cyril Chamberlain...................Alf Hudson
George Howell........................Billy Haig
Diana Beevers......................Penelope Lee
Paul Cole..............................John Atkins
Jacqueline Lewis.....................Pat Gordon
Jane White...........................Irene Ambrose
Roy Hines...............................Harry Bird
Irene French................................Monica
Lorna Henderson............................Pianist
Alan Beaton, Roy Everson, Jack Hetherington, John Payne.....................Teachers
Joy Adams, Paul Beradi, Ernest Blythe, George Holdcroft, John Smart, Pat Symons...Parents
Francesca Annis, Julia Atkinson, Josephine Bailey, Michael Barnes, David Barry, Sandra Bryant, Jeremy Bulloch,

Ted Ray

Hattie Jacques

Kenneth Williams

Joan Sims

Leslie Phillips

Rosalind Knight

Kenneth Connor

Charles Hawtrey

Richard O'Sullivan

Carol White

Cyril Chamberlain

George Howell

Diana Beevers

Paul Cole

Jacqueline Lewis

25

Nigel Bulloch, Stephanie Bulloch, Anne Chapman, Peter Cleall, Alan Coleshill, Terry Cooke, Larry Dann, Leonard Davey, Jane Evans, Daphne Foreman, Vicky Harrington, Ian Hobbs, Diane Langton, Theresa Maynard, Barrie Smith, David Tilley, Mary Weekes....................Students

Jane White   Roy Hines   Irene French

Alan Beaton   Roy Everson   Jack Hetherington

John Payne   Joy Adams   Paul Beradi   Ernest Blythe   George Holdcroft   John Smart   Pat Symons

Francesca Annis   Julia Atkinson   Michael Barnes   David Barry   Jeremy Bulloch   Nigel Bulloch   Stephanie Bulloch

Anne Chapman   Alan Coleshill   Terry Cooke   Larry Dann   Leonard Davey   Vicky Harrington   Ian Hobbs

Diane Langton   Theresa Maynard   Boy 1   Boy 2   Boy 3   Boy 4   Girl 1

Girl 2   Girl 3   Girl 4   Girl 5   Girl 6   Parent 1   Parent 2

26

Parent 3   Parent 4   Parent 5   Parent 6

86 minutes

Carol White, Diana Beevers

William Wakefield has been at Maudlin Street Secondary Modern School for 20 years, and is currently headmaster. When he sees an ad for headmaster at a new school, he sends in an application.

Noted child psychiatrist Alistair Grigg, along with Miss Wheeler, a Ministry of Education Inspector, are scheduled for a visit at the Maudlin School.

Joan Sims, Leslie Phillips

Ted Ray, Rosalind Knight, Leslie Phillips

Hattie Jacques as Grace Short

Charles Hawtrey, Kenneth Williams

27

Robin Stevens, a student, overhears that Wakefield is planning to leave at the end of term. Since the students are fond of Wakefield, the students decide to sabotage things. This, they believe, will keep Wakefield at the Maudlin school and prevent him from going elsewhere. When Grigg and Miss Wheeler arrive, the students misbehave at every turn.

Charles Hawtrey playing the piano

Rosalind Knight, Leslie Phillips

Cyril Chamberlain, Leslie Phillips

Kenneth Connor, Charles Hawtrey, Hattie Jacques

Charles Hawtrey, Hattie Jacques

Ted Ray, Rosalind Knight

Lobby Card

Richard O'Sullivan, Jacqueline Lewis

Charles Hawtrey, Kenneth Williams,
Kenneth Connor

Film Poster

Film Poster

Griggs' visit has not been useless; he has fallen for Sarah Allcock, the gym mistress, and it is obvious the feeling is mutual. Miss Wheeler is disgusted at the behaviour of the children towards the teachers. However she is softened when she visits the science master's class, where she meets the nervous science master, Gregory Adams, and feels an instinctive maternal affection for him.

Realizing his position is in jeopardy, Wakefield enlists the help of Adams to court Miss Wheeler. Adams at first is appalled by the suggestion, but after a while finds he is in fact falling for her.

When Wakefield discovers the students misbehaved to make sure he did not leave, he is touched, and promises that he will return for the next term as headmaster of Maudlin.

Ernest Blythe, Ted Ray

Kenneth Connor as Gregory Adams

Richard O'Sullivan, Kenneth Williams

Charles Hawtrey, Kenneth Williams, Kenneth Connor

CARRY ON CONSTABLE (1960)

DIRECTED BY Gerald Thomas

CAST

Sidney James.......Sergeant Frank Wilkins
Eric Barker........................Inspector Mills
Kenneth Connor....P.C. Charlie Constable
Charles Hawtrey.........P.C. Timothy Gorse
Kenneth Williams......P.C. Stanley Benson
Leslie Phillips....................P.C. Tom Potter
Joan Sims.........W.P.C. Gloria Passworthy
Hattie Jacques.........Sergeant Laura Moon
Shirley Eaton...........................Sally Barry
Cyril Chamberlain......................Thurston
Joan Hickson..............................Mrs. May
Irene Handl.................Distraught Mother
Terence Longdon..................Herbert Hall
Jill Adams............................P.C. Harrison
Freddie Mills...........................Jewel Thief
Brian Oulton......................Store Manager
Victor Maddern......Detective Sgt. Liddell
Esma Cannon.....................Deaf Old Lady
Michael Balfour................................Matt
Diane Aubrey...............................Honoria
Ian Curry..Eric
Lucy Griffiths........................Miss Horton
Peter Bennett...........................Pickpocket
Janetta Lake........................Girl With Dog
Jack Taylor..Cliff
Hilda Fenemore..............Agitated Woman
Noel Dyson........................Vague Woman

Sidney James   Eric Barker   Kenneth Connor

Charles Hawtrey Kenneth Williams Leslie Phillips

Joan Sims   Hattie Jacques   Shirley Eaton

Cyril Chamberlain Joan Hickson Irene Handl

Terence Longdon Jill Adams Freddie Mills

31

Robin Ray....................Assistant Manager
Jeremy Connor.......................Little Willie
Joan Young................................Mayoress
Dorinda Stevens.................Young Woman
Reg Thomason..................Radio Operator
Eric Boon..Shorty
Ken Kennedy....................Wall Eyed Man
Jack Hetherington ....Tied-Up Man
Peter Kelly..............................Jewel Thief
Kenneth Warren...........................Chauffer
Frederick Treves......................Announcer
Charles Stanley.................Newspaper Man
Alfred Pim.............................Newsvendor
Mary Jones..........................Radio Actress
Tex Fuller......................................Van Man
Arnold Diamond..............Chief Constable
Tom Cubitt.....................................Jeweler
Ronald Adam...............................Motorist
Paul Cole................................Barrow Boy
John Langley..........................Boy in Cart
Robert Howell...Boy
Mary Law, Margaret St. Barbe West.........
....Shop Assistants
Bill Baskiville, Frederick Davies, Arthur
Howell, Guy Mills, Joe Phelps, Jack Silk,
Robert Vossler..........................Constables
John Antrobus, Paul Beradi, Eric Corrie,
Norman Fisher, Frank Forsyth, Tom Gill,
Fred Real, Anthony Sagar...Angry Citizens

AND: Colin Gordon, Bruce Seton, Ian
Wilson

Brian Oulton

Victor Maddern

Esma Cannon

Michael Balfour

Diane Aubrey   Ian Curry

Lucy Griffiths

Peter Bennett

Janetta Lake

Jack Taylor

Hilda Fenemore

Noel Dyson

Robin Ray   Jeremy Connor

Joan Young

Dorinda Stevens

Reg Thomason

Eric Boon

Ken Kennedy

Jack Hetherington

Peter Kelly

Kenneth Warren	Mary Jones	Tex Fuller	Arnold Diamond	Ronald Adam	John Langley	Robert Howell
Mary Law	Bill Baskiville	Frederick Davies	Arthur Howell	Guy Mills	Joe Phelps	Jack Silk
Robert Vossler	John Antrobus	Paul Beradi	Eric Corrie	Norman Fisher	Frank Forsyth	Tom Gill
Fred Real	Anthony Sagar	Colin Gordon	Bruce Seton	Ian Wilson	Constable 1	Constable 2
	Shop Manager	Shopper 1	Shopper 2			

86 minutes

Due to an influenza outbreak, a suburban police station is under-staffed, and Sergeant Frank Wilkins, under pressure to maintain staffing levels, is pleased to hear that three new recruits straight from training school are arriving shortly.

Shirley Eaton, Leslie Phillips

Before arriving at the station, the three policemen are embarrassed when they learn that they have inadvertently assisted some bank robbers into their escape vehicle.

The new constables are self-proclaimed intellectual and amateur psychologist P.C. Stanley Benson, playboy and cad P.C. Tom Potter, and extremely superstitious P.C. Charlie Constable.

The arrival of W.P.C. Gloria Passworthy, with whom Constable falls in love, and Special Constable Timothy Gorse completes the roster.

Out on the street, the new constables tray their best, but unfortunately mess up a number of things. P.C. Benson nearly arrests a plainclothes detective.

Leslie Phillips, Joan Sims

Kenneth Connor, Charles Hawtrey, Diane Aubrey

Joan Sims, Kenneth Connor, Leslie Phillips

Shirley Eaton, Leslie Phillips

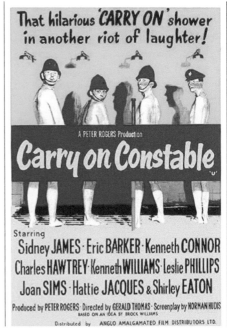

That hilarious 'CARRY ON' shower in another riot of laughter!

A PETER ROGERS Production

Carry on Constable

Starring
Sidney JAMES · Eric BARKER · Kenneth CONNOR
Charles HAWTREY · Kenneth WILLIAMS · Leslie PHILLIPS
Joan SIMS · Hattie JACQUES & Shirley EATON
Produced by PETER ROGERS · Directed by GERALD THOMAS · Screenplay by NORMAN HUDIS
BASED ON AN IDEA BY BROCK WILLIAMS
Distributed by ANGLO AMALGAMATED FILM DISTRIBUTORS LTD.

Film Poster

Sidney James, Kenneth Williams, Kenneth Connor, Charles Hawtrey

Sidney James, Eric Barker, Kenneth Williams, Charles Hawtrey, Leslie Phillips, Kenneth Connor

Lobby Card

Film Poster

Charles Hawtrey with flowers and bird

Kenneth Connor, Dorinda Stevens

Constable believes he has heard a murder being committed, but it turns out to be a radio play. Potter investigates a report of an intruder, but finds a young woman in the bath.

Potter engages the woman in a civil conversation about her recently broken relationship. Gorse, patrolling with a police dog, is unable to control the dog.

When a wages robbery takes place, they finally do something right. Benson and Potter locate the get-away car, and all four engage in a confrontation with the thieves, arresting them and recovering the money.

Commended for his efficiency and excellent results, Inspector Mills is promoted to a training position and Sergeant Wilkins is promoted to replace him. With a little help from Sgt. Moon, Charlie Constable gets his girl.

Kenneth Williams, Kenneth Connor, Leslie Phillips

Sidney James, Cyril Chamberlain, Dorinda Stevens

Kenneth Williams, Charles Hawtrey, Mary Law

Cyril Chamberlain & Sidney James

Kenneth Williams, Leslie Phillips

Joan Sims, Kenneth Connor

Sidney James, Leslie Phillips

Eric Barker as Inspector Mills

CARRY ON REGARDLESS (1961)

DIRECTED BY Gerald Thomas

CAST

Sidney James...........................Bert Handy
Kenneth Connor.......................Sam Twist
Charles Hawtrey...............Gabriel Dimple
Joan Sims..............................Lily Duveen
Kenneth Williams........Francis Courtenay
Bill Owen..............................Mike Weston
Liz Fraser...............................Delia King
Terence Longdon....Montgomery Infield-Hopping
Hattie Jacques...................Hospital Sister
Esma Cannon.......................Miss Cooling
Sydney Tafler.............Strip Club Manager
Julia Arnall....................Trudy Trelawney
Terence Alexander.........Trevor Trelawney
Stanley Unwin............................Landlord
Joan Hickson...................Hospital Matron
Betty Marsden...........................Mata Hari
Fenella Fielding..................Penny Panting
David Lodge................Wine Connoisseur
Jerry Desmonde......................Martin Paul
Ambrosine Philpotts............Yoki's Owner
Nicholas Parsons...............................Wolf
Cyril Chamberlain....................Policeman
Cyril Raymond....................Army Officer
Eric Pohlmann.......................Sinister Man
June Jago...Nurse
Michael Ward.......................Photographer
Douglas Ives.....................Fanatic Patient

Sidney James Kenneth Connor Charles Hawtrey

Joan Sims Kenneth Williams Bill Owen

Liz Fraser Terence Longdon Hattie Jacques

Esma Cannon Sydney Tafler Julia Arnall

Terence Alexander Stanley Unwin Joan Hickson

37

Judith Furse...........................Headmistress
Howard Marion-Crawford.....Wine Organizer
Eric Boon................................Young Man
Tom Clegg..........Massive Mickey McGee
Fraser Kerr...................................Landlord
David Williams........................Policeman
Jack Taylor..M.C.
Freddie Mills.......................................Lefty
Joe Robinson......................Dynamite Dan
Norman Rossington.........Boxing Referee
Anthony Sagar...................Bus Conductor
David Stoll.................Distraught Manager
Ian Curry.......................Leonard Beamish
Kynaston Reeves..................Sir Theodore
Bernard Hunter......................Wine Waiter
Jimmy Thompson...................Mr. Delling
Molly Weir............................Bird Woman
Fred Griffiths...........................Taxi Driver
Patrick Cargill...............Raffish Customer
Carole Shelley.....................Helen Delling
Ed Devereaux..........................Mr. Panting
Michael Ward......................Photographer
Ian Wilson........................Advertising Man
George Street..........................Receptionist
Nancy Roberts.....................Capable Lady
Carl Conway...............Health Club Patron
Fraser Kerr...................................Landlord
Nora Gordon..............................Cleaner
Lucy Griffiths................................Auntie
Gertrude Kaye................Lady at Bus Stop
Arnold Lee...........................Chinese Man
Madame Yang..................Chinese Woman
Angus Lennie.....................Shop Assistant
Eleanor Summerfield................Mrs. Riley
Ian Whittaker.....................Shop Assistant
S.M. Wood.......................Train Passenger
Victor Maddern, Denis Shaw...................
....................................Sinister Passengers
Eric Boon, Ernie Rice......Boxing Seconds
38

Betty Marsden   Fenella Fielding   David Lodge

Jerry Desmonde Ambrosine Philpotts Nicholas Parsons

Cyril Chamberlain   Cyril Raymond   Eric Pohlmann

June Jago   Michael Ward   Douglas Ives

Judith Furse   Howard Marion-Crawford   Eric Boon

Tom Clegg   Fraser Kerr   David Williams

Jack Taylor   Freddie Mills   Joe Robinson

Andrew Andreas, Eddie Boyce.....Waiters
Max Craig, Marcel De Villiers, Pat
Hagan, George Hilsdon, Johnny Rossi,
Jack Sharp...........................Boxing Fans
Yvonne Ball, Sylvia Bidmead, Jane Cav-
endish, Helen Frayling, Maureen Moore,
Sherry Ann Scott, Penny Service...Nurses
Wallace Bosco, John Cabot, Arthur Go-
mez, Anthony Hankey, Charles Julian,
James Lomas, John H. Moore, George
Rigby, Miles Silverton............................
...........................Old Men in Ruby Room
Mike Connor, Arthur Goodman, Richard
Gregory, Victor Harrington, Jack Hether-
ington, Fred Machon, Michael Nightin-
gale, Ernie Priest, Pat Ryan, Eric Weath-
erall..Wine Tasters
Frank Barringer, Joe Beckett, Vi Delmar,
Mabel Etherington, Peter Grant, Mu-
riel Greenslade, Vic Hagan, Sidney Jen-
nings, Norman Lambert, George Mans-
field, Fred Peck, Arnold Schulkes, Maisie
Trent, Pearl Walters....................Shoppers
Sally Geeson, Vivienne Hagger, Nicholas
Hall, Lorraine Hamilton, Kaplan Kaye,
John Langley, Linda Leo, Elaine Man-
ning, David Palmer, Lynda Reynolds,
Leslie Scoble, Teri Scoble, Gareth Tandy,
Miranda Tench, Christine Thomas............
.......................Children at Toy Exhibition

AND: Ronald Adam

Norman Rossington

Anthony Sagar

David Stoll

Ian Curry

Kynaston Reeves

Bernard Hunter

Jimmy Thompson

Molly Weir

Fred Griffiths

Patrick Cargill

Carole Shelley

Ed Devereaux

Ian Wilson

George Street

Nancy Roberts

Carl Conway

Nora Gordon

Lucy Griffiths

Gertrude Kaye

Madame Yang

Madame Yang

39

Angus Lennie   Eleanor Summerfield   Ian Whittaker   S.M. Wood   Victor Maddern   Denis Shaw   Ernie Rice

Andrew Andreas   Eddie Boyce   Max Craig   Marcel De Villiers   Pat Hagan   George Hilsdon   Johnny Rossi

Jack Sharp   Sylvia Bidmead   Maureen Moore   Penny Service   Wallace Bosco   Arthur Gomez   Anthony Hankey

Charles Julian   James Lomas   John H. Moore   Miles Silverton   Mike Connor   Arthur Goodman   Richard Gregory

Victor Harrington   Jack Hetherington   Fred Machon   Michael Nightingale   Ernie Priest   Pat Ryan   Eric Weatherall

Frank Barringer   Joe Beckett   Vi Delmar   Mabel Etherington   Peter Grant   Muriel Greenslade   Vic Hagan

Sidney Jennings   Norman Lambert   George Mansfield   Fred Peck   Arnold Schulkes   Maisie Trent   Pearl Walters

Sally Geeson	Vivienne Hagger	Nicholas Hall	Lorraine Hamilton	Kaplan Kaye	John Langley	Linda Leo
Elaine Manning	Lynda Reynolds	Gareth Tandy	Miranda Tench	Christine Thomas	Boxing Fan	Boy
Chinese Man 1	Chinese Man 2	Girl 1	Girl 2	Girl 3	Girl 4	Girl 5
Girl 6	Nurse 1	Nurse 2	Shopper 1	Shopper 2	Shopper 3	Shopper 4
Shopper 5	Shopper 6	Shopper 7	Shopper 8	Woman 1	Woman 2	Woman 3
Woman 4	Woman 5	Woman 6	Woman 7	Woman 8	Woman 9	Woman 10
		Woman 11	Woman 12	Yoki		

90 minutes

Sam Twist, Francis Courtenay, Delia King, Gabriel Dimple, Lily Duveen, Mike Weston, and Montgomery Infield-Hopping are new employees of Helping Hands, a job agency run by Bert Handy.

Business is slow; the only customer is someone speaking gibberish. Delia gets an assignment to try on a complete women's wardrobe for Mr. Delling, a gentleman who is planning a surprise for his wife. However things get complicated when the man's wife arrives home unexpectedly.

Film Poster

Foreign Film Poster

Liz Fraser in *Carry On Regardless*

Sam Twist is sent to a baby-sitting job, only to find that there is no baby, just a woman who wants to make her husband jealous. Sam winds up with a black eye.

Francis is assigned to take a pet for a walk-discovering it is a chimp and not a dog as he assumed. He takes the chimp for a walk and soon winds up at a chimpanzee tea party.

Lily Duveen is sent to a wine tasting evening, to collect invitation cards from the attendees. After she has performed this task, she samples some of the wine and gets a bit drunk.

Film Poster

Kenneth Williams, Charles Hawtrey, Sidney James

Charles Hawtrey, Sidney James, Joan Sims, Terence Longdon, Liz Fraser, Kenneth Williams, Bill Owen, Kenneth Connor

Sidney James with the girls

Kenneth Williams with monkey

After a man from Amalgamated Scrap-Iron arrives in the Helping Hands office, Bert himself goes to a hospital, where he is mistaken for a doctor.

The next job that Francis goes on is that of a photographer's model. It turns out the modeling assignment is an advertisement for a bee-keeper. He then goes on a job with a man and wife; the wife speaks German.

Liz Fraser, Joan Sims

Gertrude Kaye, Kenneth Williams, Woman

Kenneth Connor, Betty Marsden

Lefty Vincent, a boxing friend of Bert's, requires four helpers to act as seconds for his fighter Dynamite Dan. When they get to the venue, Dan is terrified by his opponent, Mickey McGee, so he pretends that he has sprained his finger. Gabriel Dimple then takes over the fight- and wins.

Film Poster

Bill Owen, Charles Hawtrey, Terence Longdon

Movie Still

Sidney James playing doctor

Miss Cooling decides on a new filing system, but things get fouled up when a cleaner knocks over a box of index cards, mixing up the assignments.

The office landlord shows up to inform Bert that he will have to vacate the premises, because he has had a better offer. When he tells the group he wants a house cleaned, they demolish it, but that in fact, gives the landlord a chance to replace it with a block of luxury flats.

Gertrude Kaye, Yoki, Kenneth Williams, Anthony Sagar

Joan Sims, Sidney James

Lucy Griffiths, Terence Longdon, Liz Fraser

Kenneth Williams having tea

Looks like Charles Hawtrey is the winner

CARRY ON CRUISING (1962)

DIRECTED BY Gerald Thomas

CAST

Sidney James....Captain Wellington Crowther
Kenneth Williams.1st Officer Leonard Marjoribanks
Kenneth Connor...............Dr. Arthur Binn
Liz Fraser............................Glad Trimble
Dilys Laye.......................Florence Castle
Esma Cannon..............Bridget Madderley
Lance Percival...................Wilfred Haines
Jimmy Thompson...................Sam Turner
Ronnie Stevens...............................Drunk
Vincent Ball..................................Jenkins
Cyril Chamberlain.....................Tom Tree
Willoughby Goddard...............Large man
Ed Devereaux.....................Young Officer
Brian Rawlinson............Nervous Steward
Anton Rodgers.......................Young Man
Anthony Sagar..................................Cook
Terence Holland.......................Passenger
Mario Fabrizi............................Cook #2
Marian Collins..................................Bride
Evan David.....................................Groom
Jill Mai Meredith.................Shapely Miss
Alan Casley.....................................Sailor
Norman Coburn............Wireless Operator
Aileen Lewis..........................Mrs. Lewis
Arnold Schulkes.................Young Officer
Emil Stemmler..............................Waiter
John Timberlake.................................Chef

Sidney James   Kenneth Williams   Kenneth Connor

Liz Fraser   Dilys Laye   Esma Cannon

Lance Percival   Jimmy Thompson   Ronnie Stevens

Vincent Ball   Cyril Chamberlain   Willoughby Goddard

Ed Devereaux   Brian Rawlinson   Anton Rodgers

Del Baker, Freddie Clark, Roy Everson....
....Officers
Dennis Carnell, Tony Hardwicke, Gerald
Paris, Cecil Paul, David Roy Paul............
....Stewards
Joy Adams, Gerry Addison, Roy Beck,
Joe Beckett, Hyma Beckley, Pauline
Chamberlain, Peter Evans, Alan Gibbs,
Richard Gregory, Pat Halpin, Aidan Har-
rington, Alan Harris, Ruth Harrison, Re-
nee Heimer, Jack Hetherington, John
Howard, Gordon Humphries, Roy Lans-
ford, Jack Mandeville, Keith Peacock, Er-
nie Priest, Jon Rumney, Pat Ryan, Bunny
Seaman, John Smart, Prunella Smith, Reg
Thomason, Eric Weatherall, Jan Wil-
liams, Ian Wilson.....................Passengers

Anthony Sagar   Terence Holland   Mario Fabrizi

Marian Collins   Evan David   Jill Mai Meredith

Alan Casley   Aileen Lewis   Arnold Schulkes

Emil Stemmler   John Timberlake   Del Baker

Freddie Clark   Roy Everson   Dennis Carnell   Tony Hardwicke   Gerald Paris   Cecil Paul   David Roy Paul

Joy Adams   Gerry Addison   Roy Beck   Joe Beckett   Hyma Beckley   Pauline Chamberlain   Peter Evans

Alan Gibbs   Richard Gregory   Pat Halpin   Aidan Harrington   Ruth Harrison   Renee Heimer   Jack Hetherington

John Howard	Gordon Humphries	Roy Lansford	Jack Mandeville	Keith Peacock	Ernie Priest	Pat Ryan
Bunny Seaman	John Smart	Reg Thomason	Eric Weatherall	Officer	Passenger 1	Passenger 2
Passenger 3	Passenger 4	Passenger 5	Passenger 6	Passenger 7	Passenger 8	Passenger 9
Purser	Steward 1	Steward 2				

89 minutes

Wellington Crowther, captain of a cruise ship, The SS *Happy Wanderer*, has five of his crew replaced before the upcoming cruise. The men, as it turns out, are quite incompetent.

Crowther is hoping to secure a captaincy on a transatlantic ship one the voyage is over. Their ports of call include Spain, Italy, and North Africa, then returning to England.

Film Poster

Passengers include Gladys and Flo, the latter trying to find a husband. Another male passenger does nothing but spend the cruise in the bar. Wilfred Haines, the chef, is continuously seasick.

Gladys and Flo both fall for P.T. instructor Jenkins, but nothing comes of it, especially as Flo turns out to be inadequate in the gym. Meanwhile, the new men try to impress Crowther.

However, one disaster follows another culminating with Crowther getting knocked uncinscious and covered in food at a party. Meanwhile, ship's doctor Dr. Binn has become enamored with Flo, but she wants nothing to do with him.

Kenneth Connor, Cyril Chamberlain, Sidney James, Kenneth Williams

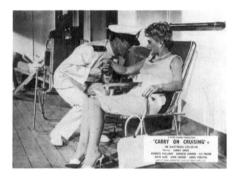

Lobby Card

Sidney James, Kenneth Connor, Ed Devereaux

Kenneth Connor, Kenneth Williams, Lance Percival

Kenneth Williams is all smiles

Film Poster

Binn gets the idea to serenade Flo with a song, *Bella Marie*, after leaving Italy, while she is sleeping. Gladys realizes that Flo is indeed stuck on Binn.

Crowther lets the five newcomers know that they have improved since the cruise began, simply by doing their jobs and not by trying to impress him.

With the help of First Officer Marjoribanks, Gladys arranges a plot for Binn and Flo to get together. It works and the confident Binn finally confesses his feelings.

Kenneth Williams, Kenneth Connor

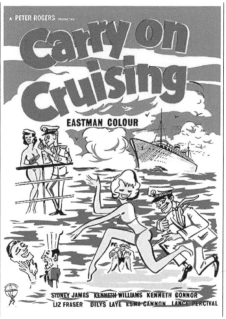

Film Poster

Sidney James, Kenneth Williams

Sidney James addresses the officers

Lobby Card

Dilys Laye & Liz Fraser

They decide to hold a surprise party for him, along with the passengers. Haines bakes a cake and the barman cables the former barman for the recipe of the Captain's favourite drink, the *Aberdeen Angus*.

The party goes well and Crowther gets his telegram telling him he has attained the captaincy of the new ship. But he turns it down when he concludes that it does not have the personal touch of the cruise ship and his crew, which he has come to like.

Sidney James, Ed Devereaux, Kenneth Williams, Kenneth Connor

Willoughby Goddard, Kenneth Connor

Marian Collins, Evan David

Sidney James as Captain Wellington Crowther

Esma Cannon playing ping pong

Dilys Laye, Liz Fraser, Kenneth Connor

Liz Fraser, Kenneth Williams

52

CARRY ON CABBY (1963)

DIRECTED BY Gerald Thomas

CAST

Sidney James..................Charlie Hawkins
Hattie Jacques...................Peggy Hawkins
Kenneth Connor......................Ted Watson
Charles Hawtrey...................Terry Tanker
Esma Cannon............................Flo Sims
Liz Fraser...Sally
Bill Owen.............................Smiley Sims
Milo O'Shea.......................................Slim
Judith Furse.....................Battleaxe Rider
Ambrosine Philpotts......Aristocratic Lady
Renee Houston................................Molly
Jim Dale..Jeremy
Amanda Barrie.............................Anthea
Carole Shelley.....................Dumb Driver
Cyril Chamberlain...........................Sarge
Norman Chappell........................Allbright
Peter Gilmore.................................Dancy
Michael Ward....................Man in Tweeds
Noel Dyson.........................District Nurse
Michael Nightingale.............Businessman
Ian Wilson...Clerk
Peter Byrne...........................Bridegroom
Darryl Kavann.............................Punchy
Peter Jesson........................Car Salesman
Don McCorkindale..........................Tubby
Charles Stanley...............................Geoff
Marian Collins...................................Bride

Sidney James   Hattie Jacques.   Kenneth Connor

Charles Hawtrey   Esma Cannon   Liz Fraser

Bill Owen   Milo O'Shea   Judith Furse

Ambrosine Philpotts   Renee Houston   Jim Dale

Amanda Barrie   Carole Shelley   Cyril Chamberlain

Frank Forsythe............................Chauffer
Geoffrey Colville...........................Printer
Patrick Durkin............................Mechanic
Michael Graham...................Boy Kissing
Penelope Lee.........................Girl Kissing
Joan Greene........................Pregnant Lady
Juba Kennerley..........Man Changing Tyre
Frank Lawless.......................Estate Agent
Joe Wadham........................Police Driver
Norman Mitchell..Bespectacled Businessman
Gordon Humphries, Ernie Rice....Cabbies
Rodney Cardiff, Warwick Denny, Fraser
Kerr, John Matthews...............Commuters
Dominique Don, Alexandra Dore, Heath-
er Downham, Joanna Ford, Marian Hor-
ton, Annabella McCartney, Olive Mil-
bourne, Amanda Reiss, Sally Ann Shaw,
Carole Shelley, Bernice Swanson, Maris
Tant, Valerie Van Ost.....Glamcab Drivers

Norman Chappell   Peter Gilmore   Michael Ward

Noel Dyson   Michael Nightingale   Ian Wilson

Peter Byrne   Darryl Kavann   Peter Jesson

Don McCorkindale   Charles Stanley   Marian Collins

Frank Forsythe   Geoffrey Colville   Patrick Durkin   Juba Kennerley   Joe Wadham   Norman Mitchell   Gordon Humphries

Ernie Rice   Rodney Cardiff   Warwick Denny   Fraser Kerr   John Matthews   Dominique Don   Marian Horton

Valerie Van Ost   Commuter 1   Commuter 2   Girl 1   Girl 2   Girl 3   Girl 4

Girl 5   Girl 6   Girl 7   Girl 8   Girl 9   Girl 10   Man

Minister   Wedding Guest

91 minutes

Speedee Taxis is a successful taxi business run by Charlie Hawkins-a workaholic. His wife Peggy feels he is spening too much time at work and not enough with her.

When Charlie is out driving his cab and misses their15th wedding anniversary, Peggy decides to get even with him. She tells him that she is going to get a job.

Film Poster

Charles Hawtrey, Leigh James

Hattie Jacques as Peggy Hawkins

Sidney James in his cab

She goes out and sets up her own cab company, which she calls Glam Cabs. The cabs are new cars, driven by good-looking young women in provocative attire.

Flo Sims, wife of a driver for Charlie, is installed as manager of Glam Cabs. Charlie continues to work with his frequently inept drivers, including the clumsy Terry "Pintpot" Tankard, whilst Peggy refuses to tell Charlie about her new job.

Although Charlie is itching to know what's going on, he pretends not to care. Peggy's company becomes a thriving success due to the large number of male taxi passengers.

Film Poster

Kenneth Connor, Marian Horton

Amanda Barrie, Renee Houston, Sidney James, Charles Hawtrey

Carole Shelley, Amanda Barrie

Charles Hawtrey, Sidney James

While Charlie struggles to cope with his wife's absences, and comes to realize what she had to endure, Speedee rapidly starts losing money and faces bankruptcy.

Peggy feels awful about the situation; meanwhile Charlie and his drivers attempt to destroy the rival company, but they are chased off. Charlie suggests a merger with his rivals, but is furious when he discovers Peggy is the owner.

Foreign Film Poster

Film Poster

Sidney James, Hattie Jacques

Girls lining up for the cabs

Sidney James, Charles Hawtrey

Kenneth Connor, Charles Hawtrey

A month later, Peggy is living at the office and Charlie's company has been broken while he turns to drink. However, when bank robbers hijack one of the Glam Cabs, Charlie goes into action.

Calling some of the Speedee drivers, the bank robbers are chased and captured. Peggy and Charlie are reconciled-especially over the fact that she is expecting a baby.

Lobby Card

Sidney James with the paper

Lobby Card

Christine Rodgers, Sidney James

Film Poster

CARRY ON CLEO (1964)

DIRECTED BY Gerald Thomas

CAST

Sidney James..........................Mark Antony
Kenneth Williams.................Julius Caesar
Kenneth Connor.....................Hengist Pod
Amanda Barrie.........................Cleopatra
Charles Hawtrey............................Seneca
Joan Sims.................................Calpurnia
Jim Dale...Horsa
Victor Maddern.................Sergeant Major
Julie Stevens....................................Gloria
Sheila Hancock........................Senna Pod
Jon Pertwee.............................Soothsayer
Francis De Wolff.........................Agrippa
Michael Ward.........................Archimedes
Brian Oulton...................................Brutus
Tom Clegg....................................Sosages
David Davenport.............................Bilius
Tanya Binning............................Virginia
Peter Gilmore.....................Galley Master
Ian Wilson.....................Small Messenger
Brian Rawlinson................Hessian Driver
Gertan Klauber.............................Marcus
Warren Mitchell........................Spencius
Michael Nightingale.........Ancient Briton
Peter Jesson.......................................Seth
Peggy Ann Clifford.............Willa Claudia
Norman Mitchell..........................Heckler
Sally Douglas....................Dusky Maiden

Sidney James   Kenneth Williams   Kenneth Connor

Amanda Barrie   Charles Hawtrey   Joan Sims

Jim Dale   Victor Maddern   Julie Stevens

Sheila Hancock   Jon Pertwee   Francis De Wolff

Michael Ward   Brian Oulton   Tom Clegg

Wanda Ventham..................Pretty Bidder
Victor Harrington...........................Scribe
Judi Johnson...........................Bridesmaid
Thelma Taylor................Seneca's Servant
Mark Hardy, Percy Herbert, Roy Lans-
ford..Guards
Gloria Best, Christine Rodgers, Virginia
Tyler.....................................Handmaidens
John Corrie, Hugh Elton, Peter Hannon,
Walter Henry, John Ketteringham............
....Soldiers
Joanna Ford, Gloria Johnson, Jane Lumb,
Vicki Smith, Donna White..Vestal Virgins
Peter Avella, Keith Buckley, Billy Corne-
lius, Bill Douglas, Peter Fraser.................
...................................Horsa's Companions
Jack Arrow, Voctor Coventry, Norman
Fisher, Pat Hagan, Gerry Judge, Pat
Judge, Cyril Kent, John Preston, Philip
Stewart ....Senators
Jimmy Charters, Maurice Dunster, Jill
Goldston, Pat Halpin, Pat Lewis, Tony
O'Leary, Laurie Rose, Frank Schock, An-
thony Snell, Reg Thomason, Rita Tobin,
Joseph Tregonino.........................Citizens

David Davenport   Tanya Binning   Peter Gilmore

Ian Wilson   Brian Rawlinson   Gertan Klauber

Warren Mitchell   Michael Nightingale   Peter Jesson

Peggy Ann Clifford   Norman Mitchell   Sally Douglas

Wanda Ventham   Victor Harrington   Thelma Taylor

Roy Lansford   Gloria Best   Christine Rodgers

John Corrie   Hugh Elton   Peter Hannon   Walter Henry   John Ketteringham   Joanna Ford   Gloria Johnson

Vicki Smith | Peter Avella | Keith Buckley | Billy Cornelius | Peter Fraser | Jack Arrow | Pat Hagan

Gerry Judge | Pat Judge | John Preston | Jill Goldston | Pat Halpin | Tony O'Leary | Laurie Rose

Frank Schock | Rita Tobin | Mo Dunster | Citizen 1 | Citizen 2 | Soldier 1 | Soldier 2

Soldier 3

92 minutes

Wile Julius Caesar invades Britain during terrible weather, Mark Antony leads the Roman army. At a nearby village, Horsa and Hengist Pod-two cavemen-attempt to warn of the invasion.

They are captured and taken to Rome, where Horsa is sold by the slave-trading firm Marcus et Spencius, and Hengist is destined to be thrown to the lions when no-one agrees to buy him.

Foreign Film Poster

Horsa and Hengist escape however and hide in the Temple of Vesta. Caesar arrives to consult the vestal virgins, but an attempt is made on his life by Bilius, his bodyguard.

In the scuffle, Horsa kills Bilius and escapes, leaving Hengist to take the credit for saving Caesar's life and to be made Caesar's new bodyguard. Meanwhile, a power struggle emerges in Egypt, and Mark Antony is sent to force Cleopatra to abdicate in favour of Ptolemy.

However, Mark Antony becomes taken with her, and instead kills Ptolemy. Cleopatra convinces Mark Antony to kill Caesar and become ruler of Rome himself.

So that they may rule a powerful Roman-Egyptian alliance together. After seducing one another, Mark Antony agrees, and plots to kill Caesar.

Jim Dale, Kenneth Connor

Kenneth Williams, Sidney James

Charles Hawtrey, Jon Pertwee, Kenneth Connor, Kenneth Williams

Warren Mitchell, Sally Douglas

Film Poster

Film Poster

Caesar and Hengist travel to Egypt on a galley, along with Agrippa, whom Mark Antony has convinced to kill Caesar. However, Horsa has been re-captured and is now a slave on the galley.

After killing the galley-master, Horsa and the galley slaves kill Agrippa and his fellow assassins and swim to Egypt. Hengist, who had been sent out to fight Agrippa and was unaware of Horsa's presence on board, again takes the credit.

Amanda Barrie in the bath

Kenneth Connor, Kenneth Williams, Amanda Barrie

Guard, Kenneth Williams, Sidney James

Kenneth Connor, Kenneth Williams, Jim Dale

Amanda Barrie, Sidney James

Kenneth Williams as Julius Caesar

Sidney James, Amanda Barrie

Charles Hawtrey, Jon Pertwee

An Egyptian soothsayer warns Caesar of the plot to kill him, but Mark Antony convinces Caesar not to flee. Instead, Caesar convinces Hengist to change places with him.

Caesar is returned to Rome, only to be assassinated on the Ides of March. Horsa and Hengist return to Britain, and Mark Antony is left in Egypt with Cleopatra.

Hengist accidentally exposes both Cleopatra and Mark Antony as would-be assassins; he and Caesar then ally with Horsa, and after defeating Cleopatra's bodyguard Sosages in combat, Hengist and the party leave Egypt.

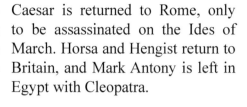

Wanda Ventham and friends

Lobby Card

Lobby Card

Film Poster

Amanda Barrie as Cleopatra

CARRY ON JACK (1964)

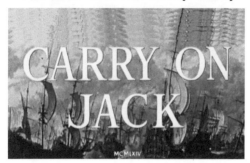

DIRECTED BY Gerald Thomas

CAST

Kenneth Williams...........Captain Fearless
Juliet Mills............................Sally
Bernard Cribbins.......Albert Poop-Decker
Charles Hawtrey................Walter Sweetly
Donald Houston..............Jonathan Howett
Percy Herbert...........................Mr. Angel
Jim Dale.............................Young Carrier
Patrick Cargill............................Don Luis
Cecil Parker........................First Sea Lord
Ed Devereaux.................................Hook
Peter Gilmore...................................Patch
George Woodbridge..........................Ned
Ian Wilson.........................Ancient Carrier
Jimmy Thompson.....Admiral Horatio Nelson
Anton Rodgers...............................Hardy
Michael Nightingale................Town Crier
Frank Forsyth.................Second Sea Lord
John Brooking ....Third Sea Lord
Barrie Gosney.....................Coach Driver
John Muzurus..................Spanish Captain
Viviane Ventura............Spanish Secretary
Marianne Stone....................................Peg
Martin Lyder......................Spanish Guard
Aileen Lewis.............................Onlooker
Josie Grant.....................................Woman
Reg Thomason.....................Naval Officer
Bill Hibbert.......................................Rating

Kenneth Williams   Juliet Mills   Bernard Cribbins

Charles Hawtrey   Donald Houston   Percy Herbert

Jim Dale   Patrick Cargill   Cecil Parker

Ed Devereaux   Peter Gilmore   George Woodbridge

Ian Wilson   Jimmy Thompson   Anton Rodgers

Kenneth Cope.................................Sailor
Del Watson.............................Press Gang
Ted Bushell, Paddy Hayes......................
...............................Surgeon's Assistants
Jack Carter, Alan Gibbs...............Marines
Frank Harper, Fred Machon, Reg Prince,
Ernie Rice.................Men at Dirty Dick's
Dominique Don, Sally Douglas, Jennifer
Hill, Rosemary Manley, Dorinda Stevens
...............................Girls at Dirty Dick's
Don Archell, Bernard Barnsley, Maurice
Bush, Vincent Fleming, Ricky Lansing,
Max Latimer, Neil Osborne, Bill Rooney,
Jimmy Scott, Bill Strange......Deck Hands
Chris Adcock, Tony Allen, Alan Bea-
ton, Joe Beckett, Jim Brady, Ernest
Fennemore, Pat Gorman, Anthony Hen-
nessey, Pat Judge, Lou Morgan, Charlie
Price, Roy Seeley, Guy Standeven, John
Tordoff................................Pirates

Michael Nightingale   Frank Forsyth   John Brooking

Barrie Gosney   Viviane Ventura   Marianne Stone

Martin Lyder   Aileen Lewis   Reg Thomason

Bill Hibbert   Del Watson   Paddy Hayes

Jack Carter   Alan Gibbs   Frank Harper   Fred Machon   Reg Prince   Ernie Rice   Dominique Don

Sally Douglas   Jennifer Hill   Don Archell   Bernard Barnsley   Maurice Bush   Vincent Fleming   Ricky Lansing

Max Latimer   Neil Osborne   Bill Rooney   Jimmy Scott   Bill Strange   Chris Adcock   Tony Allen

Alan Beaton   Joe Beckett   Jim Brady   Anthony Hennessey   Pat Judge   Lou Morgan   Charlie Price

Guy Standeven   George Hilsdon   Jan Muzurus   Maurice Bush   Max Craig   Walter Henry   Boy

Deck Hand   Man 1   Man 2   Naval Officer   Pirate 1   Pirate 2

91 minutes

Among the last words of Lord Nelson at the Battle of Trafalgar are that Britain needs a bigger navy with more men, followed by his famous line "Kiss me Hardy."

Although Albert Poop-Decker has taken 8½ years and still not qualified as a midshipman, the First Sea Lord nevertheless promotes him. He is to join the frigate *HMS Venus* at Plymouth.

He finds the crew running off to Dirty Dick's Tavern, as they are to set sail the following day. When he holds a sovereign in the air, he is mobbed by some women.

Film Poster

Barmaid Sally rescues him; she wants to go to sea to find her former lodger and childhood sweetheart Roger. When she finds that Poop-Decker has not reported to the ship yet and is unknown to the crew, she knocks him out and takes his midshipman's uniform.

Poop-Decker wakes and puts on a dress to cover his underwear, and downstairs, along with a cesspool cleaner named Walter Sweetly, is kidnapped by a press gang.

First Officer Lieutenant Jonathan Howett and his sidekick, bosun Mr. Angel, take them to the ship, where Poop-Decker introduces himself to Captain Fearless.

Foreign Film Poster

Patrick Cargill, Viviane Ventura

Kenneth Williams, Juliet Mills

Film Poster

Bernard Cribbins as Albert Poop-Decker

Donald Houston, Percy Herbert

Problem is, there is already a Poop-Decker on the ship. Poop-Decker, as a hopeless seaman, goes on to continually irritate Howett by doing the wrong thing.

After three months at sea and no action, the crew is very restless, and when they finally see a Spanish ship, the Captain has them sail away from it.

Foreign Film Poster

Film Poster

Donald Houston, Kenneth Williams, Charles Hawtrey, Percy Herbert

Peter Gilmore, Juliet Mills, Bernard Cribbins, Kenneth Williams

Lobby Card

Battleships in action

Howett and Angel make it appear it looks like the ship has been boarded by the enemy during a night raid, and using Poop-Decker as an expendable dupe to get the Captain off the ship.

Now in charge of the ship, Howett and Angel sail for Spain and plan on taking Cadiz from Spanish Governor Don Luis. However; their plot is ruined by Poop-Decker's group, who recaptures the *Venus*.

Juliet Mills, Kenneth Williams,
Donald Houston

Juliet Mills, Kenneth Williams, Bernard
Cribbins

George Woodbridge, Juliet Mills

Sailing back to England, they encounter a pirate ship, whose crew seizes the *Venus*. The Captain turns out to be Sally's lost love Roger, but upon seeing him as a coarse, brutal rogue, she no longer wants to have anything to do with him. Poop-Decker manages to escape and cut down a sail, which covers the pirates, capturing them. In Cadiz, the former crew of the *Venus* are taken to be shot, but escape with five empty Spanish men of war to England.

Juliet Mills, Kenneth Williams, Donald Houston

Percy Herbert, Bernard Cribbins, Donald Houston

Nearly home, they encounter the *Venus*. While Poop-Decker, Sally and Walter are working below decks on cutting off Fearless's badly infected leg, a fire gets out of control on deck and burns a sail. This accidentally sets off the cannons on the *Venus*, hitting all five Spanish ships. Poop-Decker and the others wind up at the Admiralty, hailed as heroes.

Percy Herbert, Charles Hawtrey, Donald Houston

Bernard Cribbins, Charles Hawtrey

CARRY ON SPYING (1964)

DIRECTED BY Gerald Thomas

CAST

Kenneth Williams.........Desmond Simkins
Barbara Windsor..........Daphne Honeybutt
Bernard Cribbins................Harold Crump
Charles Hawtrey...................Charlie Bind
Eric Barker...............................The Chief
Dilys Laye...Lila
Jim Dale.....................................Carstairs
Richard Wattis................................Cobley
Eric Pohlmann......................The Fat Man
Victor Maddern..........................Milchman
Judith Furse...............................Dr. Crow
John Bluthal..........................Head Waiter
Renee Houston...........................Madame
Tom Clegg..................................Doorman
Gertan Klauber.......................Code Clerk
Frank Forsyth....................Professor Stark
Norman Mitchell.....Policeman/Algerian Gent
Derek Sydney.......................Algerian Gent
Jill Mai Meredith.................Cigarette Girl
Hugh Futcher.............Bed of Nails Native
Angela Ellison..................Cloakroom Girl
George Curtis....................Security Guard
Nora Gordon......................Elderly Woman
Olive Gregg..............................Sergeant
Fred Haggerty...........Dr. Crow's Assistant
Tutte Lemkow...........Man in Marketplace
John Adams..............................Gate Guard

Kenneth Williams Barbara Windsor Bernard Cribbins

Charles Hawtrey Eric Barker Dilys Laye

Jim Dale Richard Wattis Eric Pohlmann

Victor Maddern Judith Furse John Bluthal

Renee Houston Tom Clegg Gertan Klauber

Philip Johns.................................Scientist
George Leech, Joe Phelps, Joe Powell......
....Waiters
Gloria Best, Judi Johnson, Virginia Tyler
....Funhouse Girls
Pauline Chamberlain, James Darwin, Ken
Lawton............................Train Passengers
Jack Arrow, Bill Cummings, Martin Ly-
der, Neil Osborne, Jack Taylor........Thugs
Cassandra Chapman, Max Craig, Hugh
Elton, Fred Machon, Lou Morgan.............
.....................................Restaurant Patrons
Anthony Baird, Patrick Durkin, John Jar-
dine, Jonathan Newth, Charlie Price...
....Guards
Marian Collins, Sally Douglas, Heather
Downham, Maya Koumani, Jane Lumb,
Christine Rodgers, Vicky Smith, Audrey
Wilson............................Amazon Guards

AND: Cyril Chamberlain

Frank Forsyth   Norman Mitchell   Derek Sydney

Jill Mai Meredith   Hugh Futcher   Angela Ellison

George Curtis   Fred Haggerty   John Adams

Philip Johns   George Leech   Joe Phelps

Joe Powell   Virginia Tyler   Pauline Chamberlain

James Darwin   Ken Lawton   Jack Arrow   Bill Cummings   Martin Lyder   Neil Osborne   Jack Taylor

Cassandra Chapman   Max Craig   Hugh Elton   Fred Machon   Lou Morgan   Anthony Baird   Patrick Durkin

| Charlie Price | Marian Collins | Sally Douglas | Maya Koumani | Diner | Man 1 | Man 2 |

Woman

87 minutes

STENCH (the Society for the Total Extinction of Non-Conforming Humans) has stolen a secret formula. The Secret Service Chief sends four agents to get it back.

They are bumbling agent Desmond Simpkins and his three trainees, agent Harold Crump, agent Daphne Honeybutt, and agent Charlie Bind. Looks like the blind leading the blind.

Film Poster

Film Poster

Barbara Windsor, Bernard Cribbins

75

The agents travel separately to Vienna, where they have traveled separately; each makes contact with Carstairs, who assumes a different disguise each time.

The quartet travels to Tangiers, where they encounter STENCH agents the Fat Man and Milchmann. Unfortunately, the agents' ineptitude results in Carstairs being knocked out in an encounter with the Fat Man.

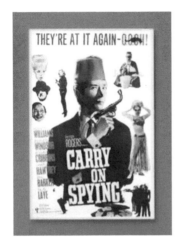

Film Poster

Barbara Windsor, Bernard Cribbins, Charles Hawtrey, Kenneth Williams

Richard Wattis, Eric Barker, Kenneth Williams, Charles Hawtrey, Bernard Cribbins, Barbara Windsor

Jim Dale, Victor Maddern

Kenneth Williams, Jim Dale

Foreign Film Poster

Film Poster

Bernard Cribbins as Harold Crump

Judith Furse, Dilys Laye

Richard Wattis, Eric Barker

Bernard Cribbins, Barbara Windsor

Bernard Cribbins, Barbara Windsor

Disguised as dancing girls in Hakim's Fun House, where the Fat Man is relaxing, Daphne and Harold attempt to steal the formula back. They encounter Lila, who has a photographic memory.

Lila memorizes the formula while the others destroy the formula papers by eating them with soup and bread. After being captured by STENCH, Dr. Crow manages to get the formula.

Spy in disguise

Kenneth Williams, Charles Hawtrey

Lobby Card

Eric Pohlmann, Barbara Windsor

Dilys Laye, Maya Koumani, Barbara Windsor, Christine Rodgers

However, the group turns the tables and escapes when Lila pulls a gun on Dr. Crow, forcing her to reverse the process. Simpkins sets the STENCH base to self-destruct before rushing into a lift with the other agents.

The lift reaches the surface, which is revealed to be the office of the chief of the Secret Service; the headquarters of STENCH was right below the streets of London! But now it has been destroyed.

CARRY ON COWBOY (1965)

DIRECTED BY Gerald Thomas

CAST

Sidney James.....Johnny Finger-The Rumpo Kid
Kenneth Williams.................Judge Burke
Jim Dale.........................Marshall P. Nutt
Charles Hawtrey..............Chief Big Heap
Joan Sims.........................Belle Armitage
Angela Douglas..................Annie Oakley
Bernard Bresslaw...................Little Heap
Peter Butterworth.............................Doc
Percy Herbert................................Charlie
Jon Pertwee................Sheriff Albert Earp
Sydney Bromley..................Sam Houston
Edina Ronay..........................Dolores
Lionel Murton....................................Clerk
Peter Gilmore.................Henchman Curly
Davy Kaye......................Undertaker Josh
Alan Gifford......................Commissioner
Brian Rawlinson...............................Burt
Michael Nightingale..........Bank Manager
Simon Cain.......................................Short
Sally Douglas...............................Kitkata
Cal McCord................Young Ranch Hand
Gary Colleano.................Henchman Slim
Arthur Lovegrove...........Old Ranch Hand
Margaret Nolan........................Miss Jones
Tom Clegg..............................Blacksmith
Larry Cross....................................Perkins
Brian Coburn...............................Trapper

Sidney James   Kenneth Williams   Jim Dale

Charles Hawtrey   Joan Sims   Angela Douglas

Bernard Bresslaw   Peter Butterworth   Percy Herbert

Jon Pertwee   Sydney Bromley   Edina Ronay

Lionel Murton   Peter Gilmore   Davy Kaye

79

Andrea Allen.................................Minnie
Gloria Best...................................Bridget
Carmen Dene.....................Mexican Girl
Jim Brady...............................Henchman
Patrick Durkin...................................Man

Alan Gifford   Brian Rawlinson   Michael Nightingale

Dave Goodey............Chuckwagon Driver
Hal Galili...................................Cowhand
George Mossman........Stagecoach Driver
Vicki Smith.....................................Polly
Lisa Thomas.....................................Sally
Donna White....................................Jenny

Simon Cain   Sally Douglas   Gary Colleano

Audrey Wilson..................................Jane
Eric Rogers........................Saloon Pianist
Norman Stanley..............................Drunk
Chris Webb................................Cowboy
Jeremy Taylor.................Master of Horse

Arthur Lovegrove   Margaret Nolan   Tom Clegg

Bob Head.......................Cavalry Trooper
Margaret Stuart......................Saloon Girl
Vi Delmar, Louise Nolan.............Women
Bill Brandon, Billy Cornelius, Michael
Stevens.....................................Horsemen

Larry Cross   Brian Coburn   Gloria Best

Jack Arrow, John Cam, Max Craig, Alec
North, Neil Osborne, Jack Sharp, Reg
Thomason........................Saloon Patrons
Roy Beck, Alf Costa, Lindsay Hooper,
Mike Jarvis, Roy Lansford, Alf Mangan,

Carmen Dene   Jim Brady   Patrick Durkin

Harry Phipps, Ernie Rice, Jack Ross,
Johnny Rossi, Fred Woods.......Townsmen
David Ashton, Tommy Atkins, Pat Baker,
Gerald Barnes, Bernard Barnsley, Doug-
las Bates, Kid Berg, David Birks, Brian

Hal Galili   Eric Rogers   Norman Stanley

Bowes, Andrew Bradford, Tim Condren,
Bill Cummings, Jack Curran, Barry De
Boulay, Billy Dean,   Reg Dent, John
Dick, Dennis Dillon, Mick Dillon, Steve
Emerson, Raymond Ford, Reg Harding,
Tony Jossa, Philip Joste, Anthony Leon,
Rick Lester, Jimmy Lodge, Eddie Long,
John McArdle, Norman Mann, Vince

Chris Webb   Bob Head   Margaret Stuart

Mooney, Bill Morgan, Richard Morgan, Bryan Mosley, David Munt, Peter Munt, Dave Newman, Raymond Novak, Richard O'Brien, Derek Pitton, Peter Pocock, Charlie Price, Michael Reeves, Tommy Reeves, Trevor Roberts, Tony Robinson, Johnny Scripps, Richard Smith, Roy Street, Chris Taylor, Rocky Taylor, Les White, Dave Wilding........................Riders

Vi Delmar   Louise Nolan   Bill Brandon

Billy Cornelius   Michael Stevens   Jack Arrow

John Cam   Max Craig   Alec North   Neil Osborne   Jack Sharp   Reg Thomason   Roy Beck

Lindsay Hooper   Mike Jarvis   Roy Lansford   Alf Mangan   Harry Phipps   Ernie Rice   Jack Ross

Johnny Rossi   Fred Woods   Kid Berg   George Leech   Cowboy 1   Cowboy 2   Cowboy 3

Cowboy 4   Cowboy 5   Indian 1   Indian 2   Man   Saloon Girl   Saloon Patron

81

93 minutes

Outlaw Johnny Finger, better known as The Rumpo Kid, rides into the frontier town of Stodge City, and immediately guns down three complete strangers.

He then heads into the saloon, killing Albert Earp, the town sheriff. Mayor Judge Burke is horrified. Rumpo then takes over the saloon, turning it into a refuge for criminals.

Sidney James as the Rumpo Kid

Sidney James, Kenneth Williams

Sidney James, Jim Dale, Kenneth Williams

Wanted Poster

Charles Hawtrey as Chief Big Heap

Marshal P. Knutt, an English sanitation worker who wants to revolutionize the American sewer system, is in Washington where he is mistaken for a real marshal, and sent to Stodge City.

The Rumpo Kid hears of the new Marshal, and tries to kill him, first with the help of Indian chief Big Heap, then framing the Marshal for cattle rustling.

Bernard Bresslaw, Charles Hawtrey

Sidney James, Percy Herbert

Film Poster

Gunflight in the street

Percy Herbert, Sidney James

Meanwhile Annie Oakley, who has arrived in Stodge to avenge Earp's death, saves Knutt from being hanged. Knutt finally runs Rumpo out of town.

When the outlaw discovers Knutt is merely a sanitation worker and not a law officer, he vows to get even with him. He comes back to Stodge City for a high noon showdown.

Indian teepees near the woods

Joan Sims, Sidney James, Jon Pertwee

Sidney James strikes a pose

Knutt conceals himself from Rumpo's gang in drainage tunnels beneath the main street, emerging momentarily from manholes to pick them off one by one.

Annie Oakley gives Knutt some pointers on how to use a gun. He does not capture Rumpo however, who escapes town with the aid of Belle, the former owner of the saloon.

Sidney James, Joan Sims

Jim Dale, Sidney James, and Cowboys

Angela Douglas well armed

Film Poster

Jim Dale, Edina Ronay

Percy Herbert, Sidney James

Peter Butterworth, Kenneth Williams, Sydney Bromley

One reviewer stated: "Watching Annie Oakley trying to teach the inept Marshal P. Knutt to handle a gun is pure comedy thanks to the wonderful Jim Dale who makes every nervous slip of the gun amusing. But the biggest reason as to why *Carry on Cowboy* is one of the best in the series is that all of those regular Carry On stars were clearly having great fun playing western characters."

CARRY ON SCREAMING (1966)

DIRECTED BY Gerald Thomas

CAST

Harry H. Corbett.....Detective Sgt. Sidney Bung
Kenneth Williams.........Dr. Orlando Watt
Jim Dale................................Albert Potter
Charles Hawtrey......................Dan Dann
Fenella Fielding...................Valeria Watt
Joan Sims...............................Emily Bung
Angela Douglas.....................Doris Mann
Bernard Bresslaw..........................Sockett
Peter Butterworth..Det. Constable Slobotham
Jon Pertwee.............................Dr. Fettle
Michael Ward...........................Mr. Vivian
Tom Clegg....................................Oddbod
Billy Cornelius.......................Oddbod Jr.
Norman Mitchell............................Cabby
Frank Thornton.........................Mr. Jones
Frank Forsyth....................Desk Sergeant
Anthony Sagar.........................Policeman
Marianne Stone......................Mrs. Parker
Sally Douglas......................................Girl
Denis Blake..............................Rubbatiti
Alec North...............................Milkman
Alexandra Dane..................Stout Woman

Harry H. Corbett   Kenneth Williams   Jim Dale

Charles Hawtrey   Fenella Fielding   Joan Sims

Angela Douglas   Bernard Bresslaw   Peter Butterworth

Jon Pertwee   Michael Ward   Tom Clegg

Billy Cornelius   Norman Mitchell   Frank Thornton

| Anthony Sagar | Marianne Stone | Sally Douglas | Denis Blake | Alec North | Constable |

97 minutes

Albert Potter and Doris Mann are courting in Hocombe Woods. When Albert searches the woods for a peeping Tom, Doris is abducted by a monster named Oddbod, who leaves a finger behind.

Albert rushes to the police station with the finger and reports to Detective Constable Slobotham, who in turn tells his superior, Detective Sergeant Sidney Bung, who has been investigating other disappearances in the same woods.

After searching the woods for further clues, the group stumbles across the creepy Bide-A-Wee Rest Home. There, they are shown into the sitting-room by Sockett the butler.

Fenella Fielding & Kenneth Williams

Film Poster

Film Poster

The seductive Valeria, mistress of the house, is made aware of their presence, and she in turn awakens Dr. Orlando Watt, her electrically charged brother.

Dr. Watt speaks to the three men, who are frightened from the house when Dr. Watt vanishes and reappears when his electrical charge runs down.

The next day, Bung, Slobotham and Potter interview lavatory attendant Dan Dann, who was a former gardener at Bide-A-Wee. Before he can tell them anything, Oddbod silences him.

A second creature, Oddbod Jr., is accidentally created by police scientist Dr. Fettle, who has given the finger an electrical charge. The creature kills Fettle, then heads to Bide-A-Wee.

Lobby Card

Film Poster

Jim Dale, Harry H. Corbett

Harry H. Corbett, Peter Butterworth

Fenella Fielding as Valeria Watt

Valeria and Watt are turning people into mannequins to sell; Bung arrives at the house to investigate Dann's death, but becomes infatuated with Valeria instead.

Potter discovers Doris as a mannequin in a dress shop, but there is no proof it is really Doris. Returning to the mansion, Bung is turned into Mr. Hyde.

Billy Cornelius, Tom Clegg, Kenneth Williams, Fenella Fielding, Harry H. Corbett

Fenella Fielding, Bernard Bresslaw, Jim Dale, Harry H. Corbett

Tom Clegg as Oddbod

Next day, Bung is his old self again, and sets a trap in the woods. Slobotham disguised as a woman for bait, is apprehended by Oddbod, while the annoying Mrs. Bung is also captured.

Jim Dale and Angela Douglas

Charles Hawtrey as Dan Dann

Film Poster

Harry H. Corbett, Jim Dale,
Peter Butterworth

Fenella Fielding, Kenneth Williams

Bung and Potter make their way to the house. When a snake fails to take care of Bung and Potter, the Oddbods are sicked on them. Reunited with Slobotham and manag-

Kenneth Williams by the cauldron

ing to return Doris to human form, they discover that Emily Bung has been turned into a mannequin.

Albert, as Hyde, overpowers the Oddbods. Dr. Watt menaces them with petrifying liquid but a re-animated mummy pushes Watt into a boiling vat in the cellar. Bung, who is unable to return his wife to human form, decides to live with Valeria.

Angela Douglas as Doris Mann

Peter Butterworth, Harry H. Corbett

Jon Pertwee as Dr. Fettle

CARRY ON DOCTOR (1967)

DIRECTED BY Gerald Thomas

CAST

Frankie Howerd.................Francis Bigger
Sidney James.....................Charlie Roper
Charles Hawtrey....................Mr. Barron
Kenneth Williams.......Dr. Kenneth Tinkle
Jim Dale...........................Dr. Jim Kilmore
Barbara Windsor..........Nurse Sandra May
Joan Sims...........................Chloe Gibson
Bernard Bresslaw....................Ken Biddle
Hattie Jacques...............................Matron
Anita Harris.........................Nurse Clarke
Peter Butterworth.....................Mr. Smith
June Jago............................Sister Hoggett
Derek Francis..............Sir Edmund Burke
Dandy Nichols........................Mrs. Roper
Peter Jones.................................Chaplain
Deryck Guyler...................Mr. Hardcastle
Gwendolyn Watts...................Mrs. Barron
Dilys Laye............................Mrs. Winkle
Peter Gilmore.................................Henry
Harry Locke.....................................Sam
Marianne Stone.............................Mother
Jean St. Clair...........................Mrs. Smith
Valerie Van Ost....................Nurse Parkin
Julian Orchard.....................................Fred
Brian Wilde........Man From Cox & Carter
Lucy Griffiths.......................Miss Morris
Gertan Klauber...................Wash Orderly

Frankie Howerd   Sidney James   Charles Hawtrey

Kenneth Williams   Jim Dale   Barbara Windsor

Joan Sims   Bernard Bresslaw   Hattie Jacques

Gregory Peck   Peter Butterworth   June Jago

Derek Francis   Dandy Nichols   Peter Jones

Julian Holloway............................Simmons
Jennifer White........................Nurse in Bath
Gordon Rollings.....................Night Porter
Bart Allison.................................Grandad
Simon Cain..............................Tea Orderly
Alexandra Dane.......................Instructress
Guy Standeven..............................Orderly
Leslie Weekes.................................Porter
Stephen Garlick....................................Boy
James Robertson Justice....Sir Lancelot Spratt
Patrick Allen................................Narrator
Ernest Fennemore, Norman Morris...........
....Junior Doctors
Harold Coyne, Renee Cunliffe, James Ure
....People in Crowd
Frances Baker, Peggy Scott-Sanders,
Philip Stewart............Audience Members
Hugh Elton, Walter Henry, Roy Lansford,
Jay McGrath, Edith Raye, Jack Ross........
....Visitors
Helen Ford, Jill Goldston, Penelope
Keith, Cheryl Molineaux, Jane Murdoch,
Anne Preston................................Nurses
Valerie Cockx, Pat Coombs, Dan Cressy,
Eden Fox, Richard Gregory, Pat Hagan,
Ernest C. Jennings, Johnny Rossi, Robin
Scott, George Spence....................Patients

Deryck Guyler · Gwendolyn Watts · Dilys Laye

Peter Gilmore · Harry Locke · Marianne Stone

Jean St. Clair · Valerie Van Ost · Julian Orchard

Brian Wilde · Lucy Griffiths · Gertan Klauber

Julian Holloway · Jennifer White · Gordon Rollings

Bart Allison · Simon Cain · Alexandra Dane

Guy Standeven · Leslie Weekes · Stephen Garlick · James Robertson Justice · Ernest Fennemore · Norman Morris · Harold Coyne

Renee Cunliffe	James Ure	Frances Baker	Peggy Scott-Sanders	Philip Stewart	Hugh Elton	Walter Henry
Roy Lansford	Jay McGrath	Edith Raye	Jack Ross	Helen Ford	Cheryl Molineaux	Anne Preston
Valerie Cockx	Pat Coombs	Dan Cressy	Eden Fox	Richard Gregory	Pat Hagan	Ernest C. Jennings
Johnny Rossi	George Spence	Man	Nurse	Out Patient	Woman 1	Woman 2

94 minutes

Phony faith healer Francis Bigger is convinced that "mind over matter" is more effective than medical treatment. During a lecture, he stumbles offstage and is admitted to the local hospital.

In hospital, he constantly complains about being mistreated. Other patients, seemingly eccentric to Bigger, appear to be getting more attention and better treatment.

Foreign Film Poster

The others include Charlie Roper, an idler who feigns illness to stay in the hospital; Mr. Barron, who has sympathy pains because his wife is having a baby, and Ken Biddle, who is courting nurse Mavis Winkle.

Dr. Tinkle, a detested doctor, and young but clumsy Dr. Kilmore minister to Bigger. New nurse Sandra May arrives at the hospital with her intention to declare her love for Tinkle.

When she enters his room (violating hospital rules that female staff are not permitted in the male quarters), Matron and Kilmore burst in on her.

Matron throws Nurse May out, and she leaves while tearfully announcing she'd rather die than live without Tinkle. Dr. Tinkle fears for his position, and wants Kilmore and Sandra out of the hospital.

Valerie Van Ost, Frankie Howerd

Kenneth Williams, Hattie Jacques

Frankie Howerd, Harry Locke

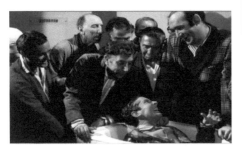

George Spence, Frankie Howerd, Kenneth Williams, Johnny Rossi, Bernard Bresslaw

Hattie Jacques, Kenneth Williams, Sidney James

Sidney James, Hattie Jacques

Film Poster

When Sandra May climbs on to the hospital roof, Dr. Kilmore and Nurse Clark assume she is going to throw herself off the roof in despair after Tinkle's rejection. Kilmore rushes to save her and climbs on to the roof.

He finds she is sunbathing, and prepares to leave, but Sandra assumes he is leering at her, and shrieks out. Nurse Clark attempts to help Kilmore before he falls off the roof, but he accidentally tears her skirt off.

Kilmore falls through a window to safety, but lands in a bath tub, where a nurse taking a bath thinks that Kilmore is attacking her. Kilmore's reputation is destroyed among everyone-except his patients.

Foreign Film Poster

Kenneth Williams, Hattie Jacques, Sidney James, Frankie Howerd, Bernard Bresslaw

Film Poster

Mr. Wrigley is invisible!

Dilys Laye, Bernard Bresslaw

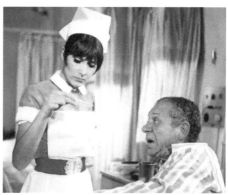

Anita Harris, Sidney James

97

Dr. Kilmore is given a hearing and with no proof to support him is forced to resign. Nurse Clark reports the treachery of Tinkle and Matron to the patients.

They all decide to exact revenge upon Tinkle and Matron, who lied at the hearing. The male patients take care of Tinkle while the females take care of Matron.

Dr. Kilmore is reinstated and appointed the new hospital registrar. Barron and his wife finally have their baby and Bigger falls down the steps on his way out of the hospital. Now he's back.

Sidney James, Anita Harris, Bernard Bresslaw

Frankie Howerd, Anita Harris, Hattie Jacques, June Jago

Hattie Jacques, Barbara Windsor, Kenneth Williams

Frankie Howerd, Charles Hawtrey, Sidney James, George Spence, Bernard Bresslaw

Sidney James in bed

Film Poster

CARRY ON DON'T LOSE YOUR HEAD (1967)

DIRECTED BY GERALD THOMAS

CAST

Sidney James..Sir Rodney Ffing/The Black Fingernail
Kenneth Williams.......Citizen Camembert
Jim Dale...........................Lord Darcy Pue
Charles Hawtrey...........Duc de Pommfrit
Peter Butterworth.................Citizen Bidet
Joan Sims.......................Desiree Dubarry
Dany Robin.............................Jacqueline
Peter Gilmore........................Robespierre
Marianne Stone........................Landlady
Michael Ward...............................Henri
Leon Greene...........................Malabonce
David Davenport........................Sergeant
Richard Shaw..............Captain of Soldiers
Ronnie Brody...........................Little Man
Pauline Chamberlain......Woman at Execution
Hugh Futcher...................................Guard
Joan Ingram..........Bald-Headed Dowager
Diana MacNamara.......Princess Stephanie
Alf Mangan..........Executioner's Assistant
Elspeth March......................Lady Binder
Michael Nightingale.....What Locket Man
Julian Orchard....................................Rake
Tina Simmons........................French Girl
Nikki Van Der Zyl....................Messenger
Otto Friese, George Holdcroft.......Aristocrats
Terence Conoley, Emil Stemmler......Servants
Jennifer Clulow, Jacqueline Pearce, Val

Sidney James   Kenneth Williams   Jim Dale

Charles Hawtrey   Peter Butterworth   Joan Sims

Dany Robin   Peter Gilmore   Marianne Stone

Michael Ward   Leon Greene   David Davenport

Richard Shaw   Ronnie Brody   Pauline Chamberlain

erie Van Ost.................................Ladies
Lee Fenton, Jacqui Harbord, Alan Meachum.....................................Ball Guests
June Cooper, Monika Dietrich, Penny Keen, Christine Pryor, Anna Willoughby, Karen Young.....................................Girls
Alan Bennett, Peter Brace, Billy Cornelius, Fred Haggerty, Lew Hooper, Maurice Lane, Martin Lyder, Fred Machon, John Morris, Norman Morris, Gerald Paris, Douglas Roe, Gerry Wain...............
....Soldiers
Peter Avella, Margaret Bracken, Jim Brady, Jimmy Charters, Eddie Dillon, Cyril Kent, Aileen Lewis, Alex Lewis, Dickie Luck, John More, Louise Nolan, Harry Phipps, Dido Plumb, Elaine Rickard, Johnny Rossi, George Spence, Rita Tobin...Citizens

Hugh Futcher   Joan Ingram   Diana MacNamara

Alf Mangan   Elspeth March   Michael Nightingale

Julian Orchard   George Holdcroft   Terence Conoley

Emil Stemmler   Jennifer Clulow   Jacqueline Pearce

Valerie Van Ost   Lee Fenton   Jacqui Harbord   Alan Meachum   Alan Bennett   Peter Brace   Billy Cornelius

Fred Haggerty   Lew Hooper   Martin Lyder   Fred Machon   John Morris   Norman Morris   Gerald Paris

Gerry Wain   Peter Avella   Margaret Bracken   Jim Brady   Jimmy Charters   Eddie Dillon   Cyril Kent

100

Aileen Lewis	Alex Lewis	Dickie Luck	John More	Louise Nolan	Harry Phipps	Dido Plumb
Elaine Rickard	Johnny Rossi	George Spence	Rita Tobin	Fanny Carby	Ball Guest 1	Ball Guest 2
Ball Guest 3	Ball Guest 4	Ball Guest 5	Citizen 1	Citizen 2	Citizen 3	Citizen 4
Citizen 5	Citizen 6	Citizen 7	Citizen 8	Girl	Soldier 1	Soldier 2
Soldier 3	Soldier 4	Soldier 5	Soldier 6	Soldier 7	Woman 1	Woman 2
		Woman 3	Woman 4	Woman 5		

90 minutes

During the French Revolution, two bored English noblemen, Sir Rodney Ffing and Lord Darcy Pue, bored with the endless rounds of country pursuits, decide to have some fun and save their French counterparts from beheading by the guillotine.

Citizen Camembert and his toadying lackey, Citizen Bidet search the countryside for the two rescuers. "The Black Fingernail" as Ffing is now known, rescues the Duc de Pommfrit disguised as an insurance salesman.

Ffing later tricks Camembert into guillotining his own executioner. Camembert is chastised by his superior Robespierre and threatened with the guillotine, unless he captures the Fingernail.

Escaping from France, Sir Rodney meets his true love, Jacqueline, leaving her with a silver locket containing a set of his mother's false teeth.

Finding out about Jacqueline, Camembert and Bidet imprison her. Using the locket as a trap, they travel to England to uncover the real identity of The Black Fingernail.

Peter Butterworth, Kenneth Williams

Lobby Card

Peter Butterworth, Sidney James

Joan Sims, Kenneth Williams

Location Scene

Camembert's lover, Desirée accompanies them. Desirée pretends to be Camembert's flamboyant sister, wearing the locket. After a series of intrigues at a ball at Ffing House, everyone's identity is revealed.

Sir Rodney challenges Camembert to a duel in order to get a head start on his journey to Paris to rescue Jacqueline. On arrival in Paris, the Fingernail discovers that Jacqueline has been moved from the Bastille.

Peter Butterworth, Kenneth Williams

Sidney James, Jim Dale

Jim Dale, Sidney James

Joan Sims as Desiree Dubarry

Film Poster

103

Ffing, Lord Darcy, and the Duc de Pommfrit travel there to rescue her. During the ensuing fight between the rescuers and the French soldiers, most of Camembert's new art collection is destroyed. Jacqueline is rescued.

Robespierre orders the executions of Camembert and Bidet on a double guillotine. However, the executioner reveals that he is The Black Fingernail himself. Back in England, Ffing marries Jacqueline.

Film Poster

Sidney James, Joan Sims

Jim Dale, Charles Hawtrey, Sidney James

Sidney James as Sir Rodney Ffing

Charles Hawtrey taking charge

Soldier, Sidney James

Jim Dale, Sidney James

Charles Hawtrey looks worried

Film Poster

Peter Butterworth, Kenneth Williams, Joan Sims, Sidney James

CARRY ON FOLLOW THAT CAMEL (1967)

DIRECTED BY GERALD THOMAS

CAST

Phil Silvers......................Sergeant Nocker
Kenneth Williams...Commandant Maximillian Burger
Jim Dale...............................Bertram West
Charles Hawtrey...............Captain Le Pice
Joan Sims...Zig-Zig
Angela Douglas........Lady Jane Ponsonby
Peter Butterworth.........................Simpson
Bernard Bresslaw...Sheikh Abdul Abulbul
Anita Harris...................................Corktip
John Bluthal....................Corporal Clotski
William Mervyn..........Sir Cyril Ponsonby
Peter Gilmore....Captain Humphrey Bagshaw
Julian Holloway...............Ticket Collector
Larry Taylor...Riff
William Hurndell...............................Raff
David Glover.....................Hotel Manager
Julian Orchard...............................Doctor
Vincent Ball........................Ship's Officer
Peter Jesson...............................Lawrence
Jimmy Charters.................Cricket Umpire
Harold Kasket................Hotel Gentleman
Gertan Klauber....................Algerian Spiv
Michael Nightingale...............Nightingale
Edmund Pegge...............................Bowler
Michael McStay.................Wicket Keeper
Joseph Tregonino..........................Servant
Renee Heimer.....................................Lady

Phil Silvers   Kenneth Williams   Jim Dale

Charles Hawtrey   Joan Sims   Angela Douglas

Peter Butterworth   Bernard Bresslaw   Anita Harris

John Bluthal   William Mervyn   Peter Gilmore

Julian Holloway   Larry Taylor   William Hurndell

107

Reg Thomason.................................Arab
Paul Beradi, Juba Kennerley.....Dinner Guests
Ernest Blythe, Muriel Greenslade, Jack Sh
arp.....................................Cricket   Fans
Simon Cain, Richard Montez, Frank Sin-
guineau...Riff
Harry Fielder, Frank Henson, Dickie
Luck, Bill Rooney.................Legionnaires
Elizabeth Counsell, Dominique Don, Sal-
ly Douglas, Gina Gianelli, Angela Grant,
Helga Jones, Margot Maxine, Zorenah
Osborne, Jo Rowbottom, Anne Scott,
Carol Sloan, Patsy Snell, Gina Warwick,
Karen Young..........................Harem Girls

David Glover   Julian Orchard   Vincent Ball

Jimmy Charters   Harold Kasket   Michael Nightingale

Michael McStay   Joseph Tregonino   Renee Heimer

Reg Thomason   Paul Beradi   Juba Kennerley

Ernest Blythe   Muriel Greenslade   Jack Sharp   Harry Fielder   Dickie Luck   Bill Rooney   Elizabeth Counsell

Dominique Don   Sally Douglas   Gina Gianelli   Angela Grant   Helga Jones   Margot Maxine   Zorenah Osborne

Anne Scott   Patsy Snell   Gina Warwick   Karen Young   Arab 1   Arab 2   Arab 3

| Bugler | Legionnaire 1 | Legionnaire 2 | Legionnaire 3 | Legionnaire 4 | Legionnaire 5 | Legionnaire 6 |

| Legionnaire 7 | Legionnaire 8 | Legionnaire 9 | Man With Fez |

95 minutes

Along with his faithful servant Simpson, Bertram West decides to leave England and join the French Foreign Legion after Captain Bagshaw brings his reputation down.

When they first arrive, they are mistaken for enemy troops, but the pair eventually enlists and are helped in acclimatizing to Legion life by Sergeant Nocker.

Lobby Card

Kenneth Williams, Phil Silvers, Peter Butterworth

Film Poster

Peter Butterworth, Jim Dale, Phil Silvers

Lady Jane Ponsonby, who has learned that West was railroaded out of England by Bagshaw, heads out to the Sahara to bring him back to England.

She has several encounters with various men-including Legion fort Commandant Burger She then meets Sheikh Abdul Abulbul and ends up becoming a part of his harem and planned wife #13.

Nocker and West are kidnapped by Abulbul after being lured to the home of Corktip, a belly dancer at the Café Zig Zig. Simpson follows them to the Oasis El Nooki but he too is captured.

Lobby Card

Angela Douglas as Lady Jane Ponsonby

Karen Young, Peter Butterworth, Jim Dale, Phil Silvers

Cast poses with camel

Bernard Bresslaw looking excited

Jim Dale, Peter Butterworth

William Mervyn, Angela Douglas,
Cricketer, Jim Dale

Angela Douglas, William Mervyn

Anita Harris as Corktip

Alas poor Yorick...

Lobby Card

After entering Abulbul's harem and discovering Lady Jane, West and Simpson give themselves up while Nocker escapes in order to warn Commandant Burger of Abulbul's plans to attack the fort.

Zig-Zig has told the Commandant about Nocker's true destination but upon his return, his story is not believed. Only when Nocker mentions Lady Jane, the Commandant realizes he was telling the truth.

West and Simpson are discovered staked to the ground at the now abandoned oasis. The relief column marches on towards the fort but discovers the attack has already occurred and the garrison is wiped out. West, Burger, Nocker, and Simpson rescue Lady Jane from the harem, leaving Simpson behind dressed as a woman. When Abulbul discovers the trick, he chases Simpson back to the fort. There, Abubul is held off and beaten. Back in England, the group reunites for a game of cricket.

Angela Douglas, Bernard Bresslaw

Joan Sims looking surly

Phil Silvers, Anita Harris, Jim Dale

Film Poster

Kenneth Williams, Phil Silvers, Jim Dale, Peter Butterworth, John Bluthal

CARRY ON UP THE KHYBER (1968)

DIRECTED BY Gerald Thomas

CAST

Sidney James....Sir Sidney Ruff-Diamond
Kenneth Williams...The Khasi of Kalabar
Charles Hawtrey......Private James Widdle
Roy Castle.........................Captain Keene
Joan Sims.................Lady Ruff-Diamond
Bernard Bresslaw.................Bungdit Din
Peter Butterworth.............Brother Belcher
Terry Scott.................Sgt. Major Macnutt
Angela Douglas..................Princess Jelhi
Cardew Robinson.....................The Fakir
Julian Holloway...........Major Shorthouse
Peter Gilmore...........Private Ginger Hale
Leon Thau.....................................Stinghi
Wanda Ventham...........Khasi's First Wife
Alexandra Dane..............................Busti
Michael Mellinger.........................Chindi
Dominique Don................Macnutt's Lure
Derek Sydney.......................Major Doma
Steven Scott.......................Burpa Guard
Nigel Kingsley........................Indian Boy
Aileen Lewis.....................Polo Spectator
Norman Morris, David Spenser...Servants
Johnny Briggs, Simon Cain, Anthony May
.....................................Soldiers
Eve Eden, Barbara Evans, Liz Gold, Katherina Holden, Tamsin MacDonald, Lisa Noble,
Anne Scott, Vicki Woolf........Khasi's Wives

Sidney James   Kenneth Williams   Charles Hawtrey

Roy Castle   Joan Sims   Bernard Bresslaw

Peter Butterworth   Terry Scott   Angela Douglas

Cardew Robinson   Julian Holloway   Peter Gilmore

Leon Thau   Wanda Ventham   Alexandra Dane

113

Josephine Blain, June Cooper, Ann Curthoys, Carmen Dene, Angela Grant, Valerie Leon, Vicki Murden, Sue Vaughan, Karen Young..................Hospitality Girls
Chris Adcock, Alan Bennion, Denis Bond, Anthony Dutton, Harry Fielder, Douglas Fielding, Dave Griffiths, John Hallam, Walter Henry, Bill Hibbert, Alf Mangan, John Morris, Phil Parkes, Anthony Pedley, Dinny Powell, Larry Taylor, John Timberlake, Patrick Westwood..
....Burpas

Michael Mellinger   Dominique Don   Derek Sydney

Steven Scott   Nigel Kingsley   Aileen Lewis

Norman Morris   David Spenser   Johnny Briggs

Barbara Evans   Vicki Woolf   Carmen Dene   Valerie Leon   Karen Young   Chris Adcock   Harry Fielder

Dave Griffiths   John Hallam   Walter Henry   Bill Hibbert   Alf Mangan   John Morris   Phil Parkes

Larry Taylor   John Timberlake   Patrick Westwood   Bagpiper   Bassist   Burpa 1   Burpa 2

Burpa 3   Burpa 4   Burpa 5   Burpa 6   Burpa 7   Burpa 8   Burpa 9

114

Burpa 1	Burpa 11	Burpa 12	Burpa 13	Burpa 14	Burpa 15	Burpa 16
Burpa 17	Girl 1	Girl 2	Girl 3	Girl 4	Girl 5	Girl 6
Girl 7	Girl 8	Girl 9	Girl 10	Man	Polo Fan 1	Polo Fan 2
Polo Fan 3	Soldier 1	Soldier 2	Soldier 3	Soldier 4	Soldier 5	Violinist

88 minutes

Sir Sidney Ruff-Diamond is governor in the Indian province of Kalabar near the Khyber Pass. The province is defended by the Third Foot & Mouth Regiment. They wear nothing under their kilts.

When inept Private Widdle is found wearing underpants after an encounter with the warlord Bungdit Din, chief of the warlike Burpa tribe, the Khasi of Kalabar plans to use this information to incite a rebellion.

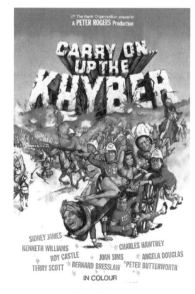

Film Poster

The British, in a diplomatic operation, fail to prove that the incident was merely an accident. ensues on the part of the British, who fail to publicly prove that the incident was an aberration.

Lady Ruff-Diamond insists that he sleep with her before she gives him with the photograph, but Khasi finds her unattractive and instead takes her to Bungdit Din's palace.

Lady Ruff-Diamond takes an inspection photo revealing other soldiers wearing underpants, and takes it to Khasi, who would then be able to unite forces and take India from the British.

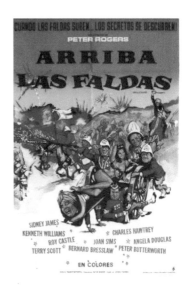

Foreign Film Poster

Sidney James, Terry Scott, Roy Castle

Bernard Bresslaw, Kenneth Williams

Peter Butterworth with the sign

Alexandra Dane, Cardew Robinson

Julian Holloway, Joan Sims, Roy Castle

Meanwhile, the Khasi's daughter, Princess Jelhi, has fallen in love with British officer Captain Keene, tells him Lady Ruff-Diamond has eloped. Some men are sent to get both her and the photograph back.

The men get into the palace, where they are pleased with the women in the harem, but are soon apprehended and scheduled for execution. Princess Jelhi helps them escape by disguising them as dancing girls.

However their disguises are seen through, so the British and the Princess run off; Lady Ruff-Diamond drops the photograph on leaving the palace.

Walter Henry, Bernard Bresslaw, Harry Fielder

Peter Butterworth, Charles Hawtrey, Terry Scott, Roy Castle

Peter Butterworth, Charles Hawtrey

Angela Douglas, Kenneth Williams

Carmen Dene, Kenneth Williams, Bernard Bresslaw

Sidney James waving

Joan Sims, Kenneth Williams

117

Returning to the Khyber Pass, they find its guards massacred and subsequent attempts to hold off the advancing Afghan invaders fail miserably.

Sir Sidney calls a crisis meeting regarding the invasion, in which he resolves to "do nothing." A formal dinner takes place while a battle rages outside.

Finally, still dressed in black tie, Sir Sidney goes outside and orders the Regiment to form a line and lift their kilts, this time exposing their lack of underwear. The terrified Afghans retreat immediately.

Soldiers defending the fort

Kenneth Williams, Bernard Bresslaw

Sidney James, Joan Sims

Call to action!

Terry Scott keeping watch

Sidney James has a cup of tea

Guests in the harem

CARRY ON AGAIN DOCTOR (1969)

DIRECTED BY Gerald Thomas

CAST

Sidney James..............Gladstone Screwer
Kenneth Williams....Dr. Frederick Carver
Charles Hawtrey.......Dr. Ernest Stoppidge
Jim Dale.....................Dr. Jimmy Nookey
Joan Sims..............................Ellen Moore
Barbara Windsor...............Maud Boggins
Hattie Jacques.............................Matron
Patsy Rowlands...................Miss Fosdick
Peter Butterworth..........Shuffling Patient
Elizabeth Knight................Nurse Willing
Alexandra Dane..................Stout Woman
Peter Gilmore...........................Henry
Pat Coombs...........................New Matron
Patricia Hayes.....................Mrs. Beasley
William Mervyn.................Lord Paragon
Lucy Griffiths............................Old Lady
Harry Locke..................................Porter
Gwendolyn Watts.................Night Sister
Valerie Leon.............................Deirdre
Frank Singuineau.................Native Porter
Valerie Van Ost...............Outpatient Sister
Billy Cornelius..............Patient in Plaster
Simon Cain............................X-Ray Man
Elspeth March.....Hospital Board Member
Valerie Shute....................................Nurse
Ann Lancaster....................Miss Armitage
Frances Baker.............................Fat Lady

Sidney James   Kenneth Williams   Charles Hawtrey

Jim Dale   Joan Sims   Barbara Windsor

Hattie Jacques   Patsy Rowlands   Peter Butterworth

Elizabeth Knight   Peter Gilmore   Pat Coombs

Patricia Hayes   William Mervyn   Lucy Griffiths

Wilfrid Brambell......................Mr. Pullen
Shakira Caine...............................Scrubba
Claire Davenport..............Wedding Guest
Heather Emmanuel.......Plump Native Girl
Frank Forsyth.............................Mr. Bean
Hugh Futcher...........................Taxi Driver
Jill Goldston.....................................Nurse
Faith Kent......................Berkeley Matron
Anthony Lang..............Sick-Looking Man
Eric Rogers..............................Bandleader
Georgina Simpson........Men's Ward Nurse
Yutte Stensgaard..................Trolley Nurse
Bob Todd......Patient on Breathing Apparatus
Johnny Wade...............................Chauffer
Rupert Evans, Mike Stevens.......Orderlies
Jenny Counsell, Jill Damas...Night Nurses
Jack Arrow, Donald Bisset, Rosalind
Mendleson, Harry Phipps..............Patients
Eden Fox, George Holdcroft, Louis Mat-
to, George Roderick, Emil Stemmler...
....Waiters
Richard Atherton, Mabel Etherington, Lee
Fenton, Alan Harris, Aileen Lewis, Alex
Lewis, Pearl Walters, Eric Weatherall........
.....................................Dance Party Guests

AND: Eunice Black, Willy Bowman, Fay
Bura, Marusa Elias, Suzanne Fleuret, Mary
Maxfield

Harry Locke   Gwendolyn Watts   Valerie Leon

Frank Singuineau   Valerie Van Ost   Billy Cornelius

Simon Cain   Elspeth March   Valerie Shute

Ann Lancaster   Frances Baker   Wilfrid Brambell

Shakira Caine   Heather Emmanuel   Frank Forsyth

Hugh Futcher   Jill Goldston   Faith Kent

Anthony Lang   Eric Rogers   Georgina Simpson   Yutte Stensgaard   Bob Todd   Johnny Wade   Rupert Evans

Mike Stevens · Jack Arrow · Donald Bisset · Harry Phipps · Eden Fox · George Holdcroft · Louis Matto

George Roderick · Emil Stemmler · Richard Atherton · Lee Fenton · Alan Harris · Aileen Lewis · Alex Lewis

Pearl Walters · Eric Weatherall · Bassist · Fat Lady · Lady at Dance · Man 1 · Man 2

Man 3 · Man 4 · Man 5 · Nurse 1 · Nurse 2 · Nurse 3 · Pianist

Saxophonist · Woman 1 · Woman 2 · Woman 3

89 minutes

Dr. Jimmy Nookey of the Long Hampton Hospital, appears to be a magnet for trouble. It all starts with an incident in the women's washroom. Nookey entered it accidentally, but nevertheless frightens a middle-aged woman out of her wits. Dr. Stoppidge wants Nookey fired over the incident.

121

During some misadventures with the hospital's X-ray machine Nookey triggers a massive short circuit in the hospital's electrical system resulting in more chaos.

When Dr. Stoppidge spikes Nookey's punch at an office party, the now drunken Nookey ends up crashing through a window on a hospital trolley.

Meanwhile, Nookey has fallen for pretty blonde film star Goldie Locks. Nookey is now being closely scrutinized by his superior, Dr. Frederick Carver, as well as the Matron.

Film Poster

Jim Dale polishing the plaque

Jim Dale, Hattie Jacques

Charles Hawtrey, Kenneth Williams

Jim Dale, Sidney James

Sidney James, Shakira Caine, Jim Dale

Meanwhile, Carver and his rich patient Ellen Moore send the disgraced Nookey to Moore's medical mission in the Beatific Islands, where it constantly rains.

Nookey discovers the local medicine man, Gladstone Screwer, who has a weight-loss serum. Nookey soon returns to England and opens a new surgery with Mrs. Moore, much to Carver's ire.

While Matron joins Dr. Nookey's clinic, Carver and Stoppidge plot to try to steal the serum. Stoppidge dresses as a female patient to effect the theft, but his luck runs out when Nookey catches him.

Foreign Film Poster

Kenneth Williams, Jim Dale, Sidney James

Kenneth Williams comforts a patient

Kenneth Williams, Jim Dale

Jim Dale, Kenneth Williams,
Patsy Rowlands

Joan Sims, Kenneth Williams

Charles Hawtrey, Kenneth Williams

123

When Gladstone learns that Nookey is making a fortune from his serum, he cuts off his supply to deliver the serum in person and get in on the profits.

Gladstone instead arrives and gives Nookey the serum, which in fact seems to cause sex changes. After everything is straightened out, Nookey and Goldie get married and the hospital staff reunites.

Jim Dale sliding down

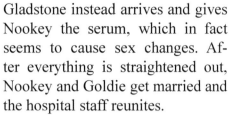

Sidney James, Kenneth Williams

Elizabeth Knight, Wilfrid Brambell

Hattie Jacques, Kenneth Williams,
Bernard Bresslaw

Sidney James and Mr. Bones

Joan Sims in fetching attire

Jim Dale, Barbara Windsor

CARRY ON CAMPING (1969)

DIRECTED BY Gerald Thomas

CAST

Sidney James...........................Sid Boggle
Charles Hawtrey.............Charlie Muggins
Joan Sims...............................Joan Fussey
Kenneth Williams......Dr. Kenneth Soaper
Terry Scott.............................Peter Potter
Barbara Windsor...............................Babs
Hattie Jacques....................Miss Haggard
Bernard Bresslaw...................Bernie Lugg
Julian Holloway.......................Jim Tanner
Dilys Laye...........................Anthea Meeks
Peter Butterworth...................Josh Fiddler
Betty Marsden....................Harriet Potter
Trisha Noble.......................................Sally
Brian Oulton.............................Mr. Short
Derek Francis...........................Farmer
Elizabeth Knight................................Jane
Sandra Caron..................................Fanny
Georgina Moon....................................Joy
Jennifer Pyle......................................Hilda
Jackie Poole.......................................Betty
Sally Kemp........................Girl With Cow
Amelia Bayntun....................Mrs. Fussey
Patricia Franklin..........Farmer's Daughter
George Moon.....................Scrawny Man
Valerie Shute.......................................Pat
Vivien Lloyd.....................................Verna
Lesley Duff...........................Norma

Sidney James

Joan Sims

Kenneth Williams

Terry Scott

Barbara Windsor

Hattie Jacques

Bernard Bresslaw

Julian Holloway

Dilys Laye

Peter Butterworth

Betty Marsden

Trisha Noble

Brian Oulton

Derek Francis

Charles Hawtrey

Anna Karen..............................Hefty Girl
Valerie Leon..........................Miss Dobbin
Peter Cockburn...................Commentator
Angela Grant...........................Schoolgirl
Gilly Grant........................Sally G-String
Iseult Richardson...Woman Carrying Tray
Michael Low, Michael Lucas...................
....Lusty Youths
Alf Mangan, David Seaforth, Tina Sim-
mons..Campers
Walter Henry, Richard Neller, Michael
Nightingale, Leslie Weekes......................
....Cinema Patrons

Elizabeth Knight   Sandra Caron   Georgina Moon

Jennifer Pyle   Sally Kemp   Amelia Bayntun

Patricia Franklin   George Moon   Valerie Shute

Vivien Lloyd   Lesley Duff   Anna Karen   Valerie Leon   Gilly Grant   Michael Low   Michael Lucas

Alf Mangan   David Seaforth   Walter Henry   Richard Neller   Michael Nightingale   Leslie Weekes   Man 1

Man 2   Man 3   Man 4   Man 5   Man 6   Woman 1   Woman 2

88 minutes

Plumbers Sid Boggle and Bernie Lugg are business partners They take their girlfriends, prudish Joan Fussey and meek Anthea Meeks to the cinema to see a film about a nudist camp.

Sid has the idea of the group holidaying at the Paradise Nudist Camp, believing that in those surroundings their girlfriends will relax their strict moral standards.

Sid easily gains Bernie's co-operation in the scheme, which they attempt to keep secret from the girls. They travel to the campsite and after paying the membership fees to the owner, realize it is not the camp in the film.

Farmer Josh Fiddler owns the land, which is nothing more than a standard family campsite located in a damp field. The ablutions are cheap and minimal.

Foreign Film Poster

Charles Hawtrey, Valerie Leon

Sidney James, Julian Holloway

Peter Butterworth as John Fiddler

The girls agree to stay, but the girls will not share a tent with the boys. Sid and Bernie soon set their sights on a bunch of young ladies on holiday from the Chayste Place finishing school.

Dr. Soaper, along with the school's matron, Miss Haggard are in charge of the girls, who include a bouncy, bubbly blonde called Babs. The girls soon leave for Ballsworth Youth Hostel.

Sidney James, Joan Sims, Dilys Laye, Amelia Bayntun

Sidney James, Bernard Bresslaw, Dilys Laye, Joan Sims

Sally Kemp, Charles Hawtrey

Film Poster

Group enjoying their popsicles

Bernard Bresslaw, Sidney James

Charles Hawtrey looks stuck

Bernard Bresslaw, Sidney James

Sidney James, Bernard Bresslaw

Betty Marsden, Terry Scott

Hattie Jacques, Kenneth Williams

There, Babs and her friend switch the room numbers on Dr. Soaper's and Miss Haggard's doors, and then tell Soaper the ladies' room is actually the men's room.

Other campers include Peter Potter, who loathes camping but must endure his jolly yet domineering wife Harriet, and naïve first-time camper Charlie Muggins.

A group of hippies arrives in the next field for a noisy all-night rave led by The Flowerbuds. The campers work together and successfully drive them away, but all the girls leave with them.

However, there is a happy ending for Bernie and Sid when their girlfriends finally agree to move into their tent. Joan's mother shows up, but Anthea uses a goat to chase her away.

Camp site billboard

Barbara Windsor, Kenneth Williams

Barbara Windsor, Sandra Caron

Hmm...Looks like a rectal exam...

Barbara Windsor and girls look on

CARRY ON LOVING (1970)

DIRECTED BY Gerald Thomas

CAST

Sidney James........................Sidney Bliss
Hattie Jacques...............Sophie Plummett
Kenneth Williams...........Percival Snooper
Charles Hawtrey................James Bedsop
Terry Scott.......................Terence Philpot
Joan Sims........................Esme Crowfoot
Richard O'Callaghan.......Bertrum Muffet
Bernard Bresslaw...............Gripper Burke
Jacki Piper...........................Sally Martin
Imogen Hassall....................Jenny Grubb
Julian Holloway.............................Adrian
Janet Mahoney.....................................Gay
Amerlia Bayntun...................Corset Lady
Lucy Griffiths.............................Woman
Mike Grady............................Boy Lover
Patsy Rowlands.................Miss Dempsey
Patricia Franklin....................Mrs. Dreery
Bart Allison.......................Grandpa Grubb
Dorothea Phillips.....Aunt Beatrice Grubb
Colin Vancao..............Wilberforce Grubb
Joe Cornelius...................Boxing Second
Bill Pertwee................................Barman
Ronnie Brody...............................Henry
Joan Hickson...........................Mrs. Grubb
Bill Maynard..........................Mr. Dreery
Valerie Shute............................Girl Lover
Harry Shacklock.........Lavatory Attendant

Sidney James   Hattie Jacques   Kenneth Williams

Charles Hawtrey   Terry Scott   Joan Sims

Richard O'Callaghan   Bernard Bresslaw   Jacki Piper

Imogen Hassall   Julian Holloway   Janet Mahoney

Amerlia Bayntun   Mike Grady   Patsy Rowlands

131

Derek Francis.................................Bishop
Philip Stone...............................Robinson
Hilda Barry.....................Grandma Grubb
Ann Way..................Aunt Victoria Grubb
Gordon Richardson....Uncle Ernest Grubb
Tom Clegg..Trainer
Anthony Sagar.................Man in Hospital
Alexandra Dane...............................Emily
Sonny Farrar...............................Violinist
Josie Bradley.................................Pianist
Anna Karen...Wife
Lauri Lupino Lane.......................Husband
Gavin Reed....................Window Dresser
Len Lowe....................................Maitre D
Fred Griffiths...........................Taxi Driver
Kenny Lynch.....................Bus Conductor
James Beck...............................Mr. Roxby
Norman Chappell.....................Mr. Thrush
Yutte Stensgaard......................Mrs. Roxby
Chris Adcock.............................Workman
Peter Butterworth................Sinister Client
Betty-Huntley-Wright....Grubb Family Member
Gerald Paris......................Train Passenger
Robert Russell...........................Policeman
Rodney Cardiff, Victor Chapman, Maurice Connor, Tina Hart, Fran Hunter, Arnold Schulkes, Reg Thomason..............
....Party Guests

Patricia Franklin   Bart Allison   Dorothea Phillips

Colin Vancao   Joe Cornelius   Bill Pertwee

Ronnie Brody   Joan Hickson   Bill Maynard

Valerie Shute   Harry Shacklock   Derek Francis

Philip Stone   Hilda Barry   Ann Way

Gordon Richardson   Tom Clegg   Anthony Sagar

Alexandra Dane   Sonny Farrar   Josie Bradley   Anna Karen   Lauri Lupino Lane   Gavin Reed   Len Lowe

132

Fred Griffiths | Kenny Lynch | Chris Adcock | Peter Butterworth | Gerald Paris | Robert Russell | Rodney Cardiff

Victor Chapman | Maurice Connor | Tina Hart | Fran Hunter | Arnold Schulkes | Reg Thomason | Man

Party Guest 1 | Party Guest 2 | Woman 1 | Woman 2 | Woman 3 | Woman 4

88 minutes

Sid Bliss runs a dating service with his longtime girlfriend Sophie Plummett. Their "Wedded Bliss" agency purports to bring together lonely hearts using computer-matching technology.

In fact however, the couples are actually paired up by Sophie. Bliss consistently avoids marrying Sophie, instead chasing seamstress Esme Crowfoot, who is also a client.

Ronnie Brody, Alexandra Dane

Sidney James gets the pie

For business reasons, and because he has no marital expertise himself, marriage counsellor Percival Snooper becomes a client of the agency. Meanwile, Sophie hires private eye James Bedsop to keep an eye on Sid.

When the agency has a mixup, model Sally Martin is unintentionally paired with the shy Bertram Muffet. Muffet was given the wrong directions to a blind date.

Imogen Hassall, Terry Scott

Film Poster

Terry Scott, Imogen Hassall

Jacki Piper, Julian Holloway, Imogen Hassall

Richard O'Callaghan, Jacki Piper

Terry Scott, Imogen Hassall

Sidney James, Hattie Jacques

Client Terry Philpott suffers several failures in his dealings with the agency including a disastrous meeting with prim, sheltered Jenny Grubb. Jenny moves in with Sally, undergoes a makeover, and becomes a model. Terry later finds romance with the "new" Jenny.

Percival's association with Sophie provokes his jealous housekeeper, dowdy Miss Dempsey, to reveal an amorous side.

Patsy Rowlands, Kenneth Williams

Film Poster

Sidney James, Hattie Jacques

Joan Sims as Esme Crowfoot

Imogen Hassall, Terry Scott, Sidney James

Mike Grady, Valerie Shute

Imogen Hassall, Terry Scott

Joan Sims, Sidney James

135

Joan Hickson looks attentive

Charles Hawtrey taking notes

Sidney James looking relaxed

Wrestler Gripper Burke, Esme's estranged lover, returns to cause havoc over an instance of mistaken identity. A sinister client, Dr. Crippen, wants a new wife. He approaches Sid Bliss, telling him his first wife died eating poisoned mushrooms, the second suffered a fractured skull because she "wouldn't eat the mushrooms."

CARRY ON UP THE JUNGLE (1970)

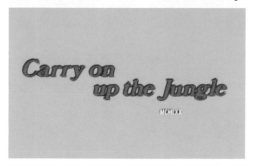

DIRECTED BY GERALD THOMAS

CAST

Frankie Howerd.....Professor Inigo Tinkle
Sidney James.........................Bill Boosey
Charles Hawtrey..............Tonka the Great
Joan Sims.................Lady Evelyn Bagley
Terry Scott...Ugh
Kenneth Connor.............Claude Chumley
Bernard Bresslaw.......................Upsidaisi
Jack Piper..June
Valerie Leon.....................................Leda
Reuben Martin.............................Gorilla
Edwina Carroll................................Nerda
Danny Daniels......................Nosha Chief
Yemi Ajibade.................................Native
John Adewole....................................King
Heather Emmanuel.............Pregnant Lubi
Cathi March, Velerie Moore.....................
....Lubi Lieutenants
Nina Baden-Semper, John A. Hamilton,
Oscar James, Willie Jonah, Jeoffrey Kis-
soon, Chris Konyils, Me Me Lai, Verna
Lucille MacKenzie, Roy Stewart, Shalini
Waran, Lincoln Webb...................Noshas

Frankie Howerd   Sidney James   Charles Hawtrey

Joan Sims   Terry Scott   Kenneth Connor

Bernard Bresslaw   Jack Piper   Valerie Leon

Reuben Martin   Edwina Carroll   Danny Daniels

Nina Baden-Semper   Me Me Lai   Shalini Waran

Lincoln Webb | Girl 1 | Girl 2 | Girl 3 | Girl 4 | Girl 54 | Girl 6

Girl 7 | Girl 8 | Girl 9 | Girl 10 | Girl 11 | Girl 12 | Girl 13

Girl 14 | Girl 15 | Girl 16 | Girl 17 | Girl 18 | Lecture Attendee | Man 1

Man 2 | Man 3 | Native 1 | Native 2 | Native 3 | Native 4 | Native 5

Native 6 | Native 7 | Native 8 | Native 9 | Native 10 | Native 11

89 minutes

Ornithologist Professor Inigo Tinkle is giving a talk about his most recent ornithological expedition to deepest darkest Africa, where he searched for the legendary Oozlum bird. He says that the bird can fly in ever decreasing circles until it disappears up its own behind. Financing the expedition is Lady Evelyn Bagley.

138

The team is led by Bill Boosey, a fearless but lecherous white hunter, and his slow-witted African guide Upsidasi. Also on the expedition is Claude Chumley, Tinkle's idiotic assistant, and June, Lady Bagley's maidservant.

The trip begins with a crazed gorilla terrorizing the campsite, and the realization by the group that they have ventured into the territory of the bloodthirsty "Noshas," a tribe of cannibals.

Joan Sims, Charles Hawtrey

The lovely Valerie Leon

Frankie Howerd, Sidney James, Kenneth Connor

Lady Bagley reveals that she has embarked on the journey to find her long-lost husband and baby son, who vanished twenty years ago. Her husband is believed to have been eaten by a crocodile.

Ugh, a bungling yet compassionate jungle dweller, has been watching the group; Ugh has never before seen any other white people, especially a woman.

Tribal natives

Terry Scott and friend

Sidney James, Valerie Leon

Film Poster

Lobby Card

Jungle native looking mean

Later, Lady Bagley is shocked to see that Ugh is wearing her son Cecil's nappy pin, and that Ugh is in fact her lost son. The next day, the travellers are kidnapped by the Noshas, but manage to bribe their way out of being eaten.

Tinkle promises the witch doctor that their gods will bestow a sign of thanks upon them. Trying to rescue the group, Ugh accidentally catapults himself into the Nosha camp and starts a fire.

Bernard Bresslaw, Sidney James, Kenneth Connor, Joan Sims, Jacki Piper, Frankie Howerd

Sidney James, Valerie Leon

Tree warning sign

Terry Scott as Ugh

Sidney James ready for action

Charles Hawtrey with pram

Ugh, June and Upsidasi get away, but the Noshas apprehend the others and prepare to kill them. As they wait to be put to death, they are rescued by the all-female Lubby-Dubby tribe led by the gorgeous Leda. Leda takes them to the lost world of Aphrodisia, where tribal king Tonka turns out to be none other than Lady Bagley's missing husband Walter Bagley.

Sidney James, Kenneth Connor, Frankie Howerd, Bernard Bresslaw

Sidney James, Valerie Leon

Sidney James, Joan Sims

Joan Sims, Frankie Howerd

Lobby Card

CARRY ON AT YOUR CONVENIENCE (1971)

DIRECTED BY GERALD THOMAS

CAST

Sidney James........................Sid Plummer
Kenneth Williams.................W.C. Boggs
Charles Hawtrey................Charles Coote
Joan Sims...........................Chloe Moore
Hattie Jacques................Beattie Plummer
Bernard Bresslaw.................Bernie Hulke
Kenneth Cope.......................Vic Spanner
Patsy Rowlands..........Hortense Withering
Jacki Piper......................Myrtle Plummer
Richard O'Callaghan............Lewis Boggs
Bill Maynard...........................Fred Moore
Davy Kaye.......................................Benny
Renee Houston.................Agatha Spanner
Marianne Stone...............................Maud
Margaret Nolan...............................Popsy
Geoffrey Hughes..............................Willie
Hugh Futcher.....................................Ernie
Simon Cain....................................Barman
Leon Greene......................................Chef
Harry Towb.....................................Doctor
Peter Burton.......................Hotel Manager
Larry Martyn..............Rifle Range Owner
Shirley Stelfox..................Bunny Waitress
Alec Bregonzi.....................Photographer
Bill Pertwee...........Whippet Inn Manager
Terry Scott...............................Mr. Allcock
Philip Stone........................Mr. Bulstrode

Sidney James   Kenneth Williams   Charles Hawtrey

Joan Sims   Hattie Jacques   Bernard Bresslaw

Kenneth Cope   Patsy Rowlands   Jacki Piper

Richard O'Callaghan   Bill Maynard   Davy Kaye

Renee Houston   Marianne Stone   Margaret Nolan

Amelia Bayntun......................Mrs. Spragg
Duncan Flanning..........Middle-Class Gent
Tina Hart..................................Usherette
Anouska Hempel...........New Canteen Girl
Walter Henry......................Cinema Patron
Julian Holloway................................Roger
Lindsay Hooper......................Hotel Guest
Jack Ross...........................Cinema Cashier
Fred Woods.........................Strike Breaker
Peter Avella, Kid Berg, Jim Brady, Michael Buck, John Clements, Maurice Dunster, Jill Goldston, Bill Hibbert, George Hilsdon, Cyril Kent, Roland Oliver, Phil Parkes, Lenny Piper, Bob Ramsey, Jack Sharp, Barry Summerford..Factory Workers

Geoffrey Hughes   Hugh Futcher   Simon Cain

Leon Greene   Harry Towb   Peter Burton

Larry Martyn   Amelia Bayntun   Tina Hart

Anouska Hempel   Walter Henry   Julian Holloway   Lindsay Hooper   Jack Ross   Fred Woods   Peter Avella

Kid Berg   Jim Brady   Jill Goldston   Bill Hibbert   George Hilsdon   Cyril Kent   Phil Parkes

Lenny Piper   Bob Ramsey   Jack Sharp   Barry Summerford   Mo Dunster   Factory Worker 1   Factory Worker 2

Man 1   Man 2   Man 3   Man 4   Man 5   Man 6   Man 7

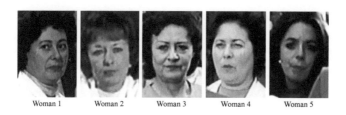

| Woman 1 | Woman 2 | Woman 3 | Woman 4 | Woman 5 |

90 minutes

W.C. Boggs, owner of bathroom ceramics factory W.C. Boggs & Son, is having a bit of trouble. Vic Spanner, a lazy union rep, continually stirs up trouble in the works, to the annoyance of both his co-workers and the management.

Spanner calls strikes at the drop of a hat, usually for no reason except a minor incident or merely because he wants time off to attend a local football match.

Site foreman Sid Plummer bridges the gap between workers and management, keeping the place going despite Spanner's strikes for no legitimate reason.

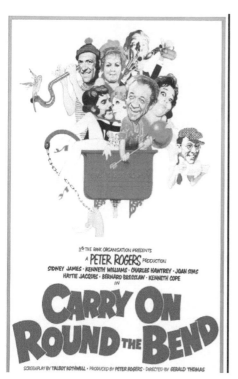

Alternate Film Poster

Richard O'Callaghan, Jacki Piper

Kenneth Williams, Richard O'Callaghan

145

Prissy product designer Charles Coote has included a bidet in his latest designs, but Boggs objects to the manufacture of such things, which he says are dubious.

W.C. will not change his stance even after his son, Lewis Boggs, secures a large overseas order for the bidets. It is a deal that could save the struggling firm, which W.C. has to admit is in debt to the banks.

Bernie Hulke, Spanner's right-hand man, is in love with Sid's daughter, factory canteen worker Myrtle, but also in the running for her affections is Lewis.

Sid enjoys a relationship with his neighbour, Chloe Moore, a neglected wife. Sid's own wife Beattie is lazy, spending most of her time trying to teach her pet bird to talk.

Bernard Bresslaw, Sidney James,
Kenneth Cope

Kenneth Williams, Patsy Rowlands

Charles Hawtrey as Charles Coote

Bernard Bresslaw, Kenneth Cope

Sid and Beattie find that Joey the budgie can correctly predict winners of horse races– he tweets when the horse's name is read out. Sid bets on Joey's tips and makes several large wins, helping Boggs in the process.

The men-who had been on strike-finally return to work, but only to attend the annual coach trip to Brighton. Everyone gets along fine-a lot of liquor is flowing.

Film Poster

Lobby Card

Charles Hawtrey, Sidney James

Sidney James, Richard O'Callaghan, Charles Hawtrey

Renee Houston with fashionable hairdo

Joan Sims as Chloe Moore

Sidney James sits alone

Richard O'Callaghan, Kenneth Williams,
Sidney James

Hattie Jacques near the birdcage

Joan Sims, Sidney James,
Kenneth Williams

Patsy Rowlands, Kenneth Williams

Kenneth Cope with little red book

Boggs, now fully lubricated, takes up with his faithful, adoring secretary, Hortense Withering. Lewis Boggs manages to win Myrtle from Vic Spanner after giving Vic a thrashing.

Vic later gets a public spanking by his mother when the group returns to the factory. There, the workers and management pull together to produce the big bidet order to save the company.

148

CARRY ON HENRY (1971)

DIRECTED BY GERALD THOMAS

CAST

Sidney James.................King Henry VIII
Kenneth Williams........Thomas Cromwell
Charles Hawtrey...Sir Roger de Lodgerley
Joan Sims.............................Queen Marie
Terry Scott.......................Cardinal Wolsey
Barbara Windsor...........................Bettina
Kenneth Connor...Lord Hampton of Wick
Julian Holloway......................Sir Thomas
Peter Gilmore.......King Francis of France
Julian Orchard...............Duc de Poncenay
Gertan Klauber.................................Bidet
Peter Butterworth....Charles, Earl of Bristol
David Davenport.................Major Domo
Margaret Nolan....................Buxom Lass
William Mervyn.......................Physician
Milton Reid...........................Executioner
Norman Chappell.................First Plotter
Douglas Ridley.................Second Plotter
Derek Francis...............................Farmer
Bill Maynard.........................Guy Fawkes
David Prowse...............Bearded Torturer
Monika Dietrich..........Katherine Howard
Marjir Lawrence.................Serving Maid
Patsy Rowlands..............................Queen
Billy Cornelius...............................Guard
Alan Curtis..........................Conte di Pisa
John Bluthal.........................Royal Tailor

Sidney James · Kenneth Williams · Charles Hawtrey

Joan Sims · Terry Scott · Barbara Windsor

Kenneth Connor · Julian Holloway · Peter Gilmore

Julian Orchard · Gertan Klauber · Peter Butterworth

David Davenport · Margaret Nolan · William Mervyn

Raymond Ford....................French Knight
Bill McGuirk..............................Flunkey
John Doye, Roy Everson.................Lords
Les Clark, Mike Stevens....Men With Dogs
Leon Greene, Harold Sanderson..Torturers
Micky Clarke, Dave Murphy, Robert Putt
....Servants
Barry De Boulay, David Dillon, Mick Dillon...Little Men
Vic Armstrong, Jimmy Lodge, Colin
Skeaping, Tony Smart, Gerry Wain..........
....Riders
Harry Fielder, Alan Harris, Bill Hibbert, Lou
Morgan, Terence Mountain, Gerald Paris
....Guards
Warwick Denny, Otto Friese, Irene Harrison, Aileen Lewis, Pat Lewis, Peter Munt,
Peter Rigby, Trevor Roberts....Courtiers

Milton Reid   Norman Chappell   Douglas Ridley

Derek Francis   Bill Maynard   David Prowse

Monika Dietrich   Marjir Lawrence   Patsy Rowlands

Billy Cornelius   Alan Curtis   John Bluthal

John Doye   Roy Everson   Mike Stevens   Leon Greene   Harold Sanderson   Dave Murphy   Bill Hibbert

Lou Morgan   Gerald Paris   Warwick Denny   Otto Friese   Irene Harrison   Aileen Lewis   Pat Lewis

Guard 1   Guard 2   Guard 3   Guard 4   Lord   Man 1   Man 2

| Man 3 | Man 4 | Man 5 | Man 6 | Man 7 | Musician 1 | Musician 2 |

| Servant | Soldier 1 | Soldier 2 | Soldier 3 | Woman 1 | Woman 2 |

89 minutes

This film is based on a recently discovered manuscript by one William Cobbler, which reveals that Henry VIII did in fact have two more wives. Although it was first thought that Cromwell originated the story, it is now known to be definitely all Cobbler's... from beginning to end. Henry VIII has his wife beheaded and quickly marries Marie of Normandy. This union was orchestrated by Cardinal Wolsey; Marie is cousin of King Francis of France.

Charles Hawtrey, Sidney James,
Kenneth Williams

Sidney James as Henry VIII

Foreign Film Poster

151

Henry's wedding night ardour dampens when he finds Marie reeks of garlic, but she refuses to stop eating it. Marie gets frustrated at Henry's lack of attention.

Bettina is the daughter of the Earl of Bristol. Assisting to get rid of Marie is Thomas Cromwell, who has the king kidnapped by Lord Hampton of Wick.

She soon receives amorous advances from Sir Roger de Lodgerley. Henry is happy to be rid of Marie, especially since he has found a new paramour-the lovely Bettina.

Terry Scott, Kenneth Williams

Film Poster

Sidney James, Joan Sims

Charles Hawtrey, Joan Sims

Sidney James, Joan Sims

Lobby Card

Cromwell and Lord Hampton also secretly plot to bring the king to harm as part of this escapade, but the false kidnapping fails, and Henry is unharmed.

Henry seizes on Marie's infidelity with de Lodgerley to be free of her; all he needs is a confession from de Lodgerley. He orders Cromwell to extract a confession using any means necessary.

Film Poster

Kenneth Williams, Sidney James,
Terry Scott

Kenneth Connor, Bill Maynard,
Norman Chappell

Norman Chappell, Kenneth Connor,
Sidney James

Sidney James, Kenneth Williams

Sidney James, Peter Gilmore

153

This leads to a session in the torture chamber, where Henry keeps changing his mind about the confession due to political necessities, requiring multiple changes and retractions of the original confession. Wolsey is baffled by all the intrigue, and Cromwell is driven to treason by all of Henry's unreasonable demands.

Sidney James, Joan Sims

Film Poster

Sidney James, Barbara Windsor, Gerald Thomas, Joan Sims, Julian Holloway

Sidney James, Barbara Windsor

Joan Sims, Sidney James

Terry Scott, Patsy Rowlands

CARRY ON ABROAD (1972)

DIRECTED BY GERALD THOMAS

CAST

Sidney James............................Vic Flange
Kenneth Williams.............Stuart Farquhar
Charles Hawtrey.................Eustace Tuttle
Joan Sims...............................Cora Flange
Bernard Bresslaw...........Brother Bernard
Barbara Windsor................Sadie Tomkins
Kenneth Connor...................Stanley Blunt
Peter Butterworth.............................Pepe
Jimmy Logan.......................Bert Conway
June Whitfield.....................Evelyn Blunt
Hattie Jacques..................................Floella
Derek Francis...................Brother Martin
Sally Geeson.......................................Lily
Ray Brooks....................................Giorgio
Carol Hawkins...............................Marge
John Clive..Robin
Jack Douglas....................................Harry
Patsy Rowlands.....................Miss Dobbs
Gail Grainger....................Moira Plunkett
David Kernan............................Nicholas
Amelia Bayntun.....................Mrs. Tuttle
Alan Curtis............................Police Chief
Gertan Klauber.................Postcard Seller
Hugh Futcher...............................Jailer
Olga Lowe...........................Madame Fifi
Bill Maynard.......................Mr. Fiddler
Terry Scott.......................Irate Customer

Sidney James   Kenneth Williams   Charles Hawtrey

Joan Sims   Bernard Bresslaw   Barbara Windsor

Kenneth Connor   Peter Butterworth   Jimmy Logan

June Whitfield   Hattie Jacques   Derek Francis

Sally Geeson   Ray Brooks   Carol Hawkins

155

Josie Grant................................Prostitute
Lindsay Marsh.........................Air Hostess
Joseph Tregonino......................Workman
Walter Henry, Brian Osborne, Phil Parkes
....Stall Holders
Alan Harris, Bill Hibbert, Mike Reynell
....Holiday-Makers
Tony Allen, Peter Dukes, Harry Fielder,
Alan Meachum, Gerald Paris, Robert
Smythe, Mike Stevens....................Monks

John Clive   Jack Douglas   Patsy Rowlands

Gail Grainger   David Kernan   Amelia Bayntun

Alan Curtis   Gertan Klauber   Hugh Futcher   Olga Lowe   Josie Grant   Joseph Tregonino   Walter Henry

Brian Osborne   Phil Parkes   Alan Harris   Bill Hibbert   Mike Reynell   Tony Allen   Peter Dukes

Harry Fielder   Alan Meachum   Gregory Peck   Gerald Paris   Mike Stevens   Man 1   Man 2

Man 3   Man 4   Man 5   Man 6   Man 7   Woman 1   Woman 2

88 minutes

Pub landlord and frequent holiday-maker Vic Flange openly flirts with widow Sadie Tompkins as Vic's wife, Cora watches disdainfully. Friend Harry lets it slip that Sadie is going to be included in an upcoming holiday.

156

The package holiday is a trip to the island of Elsbels, in the Mediterranean. When Cora discovers Sadie is coming along, she is furious.

Cora, who avoids holidays because she hates flying, suddenly decides to accompany her husband on the trip, to make sure he keeps away from Sadie.

Wundatours Travel Agency representative Stuart Farquhar, along with secretary Moira Plunkett, welcome the passengers. Among them are the henpecked Stanley Blunt and his overbearing wife Evelyn; drunken mama's boy Eustace Tuttle; and brash Scotsman Bert Conway.

Joan Sims as Cora Flange

The cast of Carry On Abroad

Sidney James, Joan Sims

June Whitfield, Kenneth Connor

Gail Grainger, Kenneth Williams, Barbara Windsor

Peter Butterworth, Kenneth Connor

157

Young and lovely friends Lily and Marge, who are each hoping to find a man to fall in love with are also along, as well as a party of monks, including the timid Brother Bernard. When they arrive they discover their hotel is only half-finished. Manager Pepe desperately tries to run the place, but the hotel also has a number of faults and Pepe is soon overrun with complaints.

In spite of the numerous problems they encounter, Farquhar is determined that everyone should have a good time. Dinner gets burned; when the windows are opened, mosquitos pour into the hotel.

Meanwhile Marge takes a liking to Brother Bernard, while Lily lures the dashing Nicholas away from his friend. Stanley attempts to seduce Cora while his wife is absent, but she is more interested in keeping Vic away from Sadie.

Kenneth Williams, Gail Grainger, Bill Maynard

Barbara Windsor, Jimmy Logan

Gail Grainger, Kenneth Williams

Foreign Film Poster

158

Joan Sims, Sidney James, Carol Hawkins, Sally Geeson

Sally Geeson, Sidney James, Carol Hawkins

Film Poster

I can't stand the noise!

Sidney James, Joan Sims, Jack Douglas

A little wine in the bathtub

The next day, the builders return; Vic discovers a local brew that blesses the drinker with X-ray vision and he is able to see through women's clothing.

In the local prison, Miss Plunkett seduces the Chief of Police, and the tourists are released after having been arrested for causing a disturbance at a brothel.

The last night in the hotel starts as a success, with all the guests at ease with each other thanks to the punch being spiked with Santa Cecelia's elixir.

During a rainstorm, the hotel begins to collapse. Later we see an Elsbels reunion at Vic & Cora's pub. Farquhar has also lost his job at Wundatours and started working at the pub.

Sidney James offers Joan Sims an eggroll

Gail Grainger, Kenneth Williams, Peter Butterworth

Sidney James, Olga Lowe

Gertan Klauber, Kenneth Williams

CARRY ON MATRON (1972)

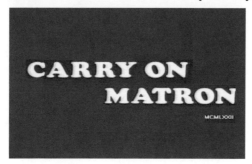

DIRECTED BY Gerald Thomas

CAST

Sidney James.............................Sid Carter
Hattie Jacques...............................Matron
Kenneth Williams......Sir Bernard Cutting
Charles Hawtrey......Dr. Francis A. Goode
Joan Sims.............................Mrs. Tidey
Bernard Bresslaw..................Ernie Bragg
Kenneth Cope.......................Cyril Carter
Terry Scott.................................Dr. Prodd
Barbara Windsor.......Nurse Susan Connor
Kenneth Connor.......................Mr. Tidey
Jacki Piper...................................Sister
Bill Maynard................................Freddy
Patsy Rowlands.................Evelyn Banks
Derek Francis................................Arthur
Amelia Bayntun...................Mrs. Jenkins
Valerie Leon.........................Jane Darling
Brian Osborne.............Ambulance Driver
Gwendolyn Watts...............Frances Kemp
Valerie Shute....................Miss Smethurst
Margaret Nolan.....................Mrs. Tucker
Michael Nightingale...................Pearson
Wendy Richard.....................Miss Willing
Zena Clifton...........................Au Pair Girl
Bill Kenwright.............................Reporter
Robin Hunter.........................Mr. Darling
Jack Douglas..................Twitching Father
Madeline Smith.......................Miss Pullitt

Sidney James

Hattie Jacques

Kenneth Williams

Charles Hawtrey

Joan Sims

Bernard Bresslaw

Kenneth Cope

Terry Scott

Barbara Windsor

Kenneth Connor

Jacki Piper

Bill Maynard

Patsy Rowlands

Derek Francis

Amelia Bayntun

161

Juliet Harmer......................Mrs. Bentley
Rodney Cardiff......................Outpatient
Shirley English..............Lady in Hospital
Alan Harris......................Photographer
Walter Henry, Bill Westley.....................
.....................................Wedding Guests

Valerie Leon

Brian Osborne

Gwendolyn Watts

Shakira Caine, Angela Cheyne, Laura
Collins, Jill Goldston, Gilly Grant, Eliz-
abeth Knight, Lindsay Marsh, Lesley
North, Tina Simmons, Yutte Stensgaard....
.... Nurses

Valerie Shute   Margaret Nolan   Michael Nightingale

Wendy Richard   Zena Clifton   Bill Kenwright

Robin Hunter   Jack Douglas   Madeline Smith   Rodney Cardiff   Alan Harris   Walter Henry   Bill Westley

Shakira Caine   Jill Goldston   Gilly Grant   Elizabeth Knight   Lindsay Marsh   Tina Simmons   Yutte Stensgaard

Man   Nurse 1   Nurse 2   Nurse 3   Patient   Woman 1   Woman 2

87 minutes

Sid Carter is the cunning head of a criminal gang that includes the long-haired drip Ernie Bragg, the cheeky Freddy and Carter's honest son, Cyril.

Sidney James, Bill Maynard

Cyril does not want a life of crime, but is blackmailed emotionally by his father into going along with his scheme to rob Finisham Maternity Hospital for its stock of contraceptive pills and sell them abroad.

Cyril disguises himself as a new female nurse to look over the hospital. Assumed to be one of the new student nurses who have just arrived, he is assigned to share a room with Susan Ball, a shapely blonde nurse.

Unfortunately for Cyril, he also catches the eye of the hospital ladies' man, Dr. Prodd. Hypochondriac registrar Sir Bernard Cutting is convinced he's undergoing a sex change.

Cast picture of *Carry On Matron*

Kenneth Cope, Sidney James

Sidney James, Kenneth Cope

Charles Hawtrey, Kenneth Williams

Hattie Jacques, Jacki Piper

Kenneth Williams, Michael Nightingale

When he consults the Dr. F.A. Goode, Goode dishes out psychiatric claptrap, stating that Cutting merely wants to prove his manhood, and Cutting decides he is in love with Matron.

Matron has more than enough to deal with in the wards, with the gluttonous Mrs. Tidey, who seems more interested in eating than producing a baby.

Film Poster

Foreign Film Poster

Lobby Card

Lobby Card

Kenneth Cope, Bernard Bresslaw, Sidney James, Bill Maynard, Hattie Jacques, Kenneth Williams

Kenneth Cope, Sidney James

Sidney James, Gwendolyn Watts

Film Poster

Hattie Jacques, Charles Hawtrey

Sidney James on the phone

When Cyril goes back to Prodd's room to get a hospital map, Prodd tries to get fresh with him. But they are called out to attend film star Jane Darling, about to give birth to triplets.

After Cyril knocks Prodd out in the ambulance, he is forced to deal with the birth by himself. Jane Darling is delighted with Cyril, who is hailed a heroine-bringing glory to the hospital.

Susan uncovers Cyril's disguise, but, having fallen in love with him, keeps quiet. Meanwhile, Sid and his gang enter the hospital in disguise, but their plans are thwarted by some expectant mothers.

When the hospital is about to call the police, Sid reveals Cyril is in fact a man-something that would bring humiliation and ridicule on the hospital if it came out.

Hattie Jacques, Kenneth Williams, Bernard Bresslaw

Joan Sims, Hattie Jacques

Hattie Jacques as Matron

CARRY ON GIRLS (1973)

DIRECTED BY Gerald Thomas

CAST

Sidney James......................Sidney Fiddler
Barbara Windsor.................Hope Springs
Joan Sims........................Connie Philpotts
Kenneth Connor......Mayor Frederick Bumble
Bernard Bresslaw.......Peter/Patricia Potter
June Whitfield..........Augusta Prodworthy
Peter Butterworth........................Admiral
Jack Douglas................................William
Patsy Rowlands..............Mildred Bumble
Joan Hickson.........................Mrs. Dukes
David Lodge...................Police Inspector
Valerie Leon.......................Patricia Potter
Margaret Nolan...................Dawn Brakes
Sally Geeson...................................Debra
Patricia Franklin.......................Rosemary
Brian Osborne........................First Citizen
Bill Pertwee............................Fire Chief
Marianne Stone.......................Miss Drew
Wendy Richard........................Ida Downs
Robin Askwith..............Larry Prodworthy
Jimmy Logan...................Cecil Gaybody
Arnold Ridley...................Alderman Pratt
Brenda Cowling............................Matron
Angela Grant........................Miss Bangor
Billy Cornelius...................................P.C.
Michael Nightingale....City Gent on Tube
Laraine Humphrys...............Eileen Denby

Sidney James   Barbara Windsor   Joan Sims

Kenneth Connor   Bernard Bresslaw   June Whitfield

Peter Butterworth   Jack Douglas   Patsy Rowlands

Joan Hickson   David Lodge   Valerie Leon

Margaret Nolan   Sally Geeson   Patricia Franklin

Zena Clifton..........................Susan Brooks
Shirley English..................Woman Libber
Jim Tyson................Beauty Contest Judge
Cy Town..............................Photographer
Pauline Peart........................Gloria Winch
Barbara Wise............................Julia Oates
Carol Wyler.......................Maureen Darcy
Caroline Whitaker..................Mary Parker
Fred Peck.............................Man On Tube
Mavis Fyson........................Frances Cake
Elsie Winsor...............................Tea Lady
Paul Chapman.........................Sound Man
Aileen Lewis, Alex Lewis, Reg Thomason, Philip Webb...........Council Members
Ernest Blythe, Pat Hagan, Edward Palmer, Pat Ryan, Philip Stewart..Hotel Guests
Sean Barry, Hyma Beckley, Kid Berg, Daniel Brown, Jimmy Charters, Billy Davis, Eddie Dillon, John Emms, Roy Everson, Hugh Futcher, Iris Fry, Alan Gill, Victor Harrington, Pat Harrison, Ernest C. Jennings, David McGillivray, Alf Mangan, Alan Meachum, Bob Ramsey, Ian Selby, Larry Sheppard, John Smart, Ron Tarr, Rita Tobin, Joseph Tregonino, Mike Varey, Fred Woods.....Audience Members

Brian Osborne

Bill Pertwee

Marianne Stone

Wendy Richard

Robin Askwith

Jimmy Logan

Arnold Ridley

Brenda Cowling

Angela Grant

Billy Cornelius

Michael Nightingale   Laraine Humphrys

Zena Clifton

Shirley English

Jim Tyson

Cy Town

Pauline Peart

Barbara Wise

Carol Wyler

Caroline Whitaker

Fred Peck

Mavis Fyson

Elsie Winsor

Paul Chapman

Aileen Lewis

168

Alex Lewis   Reg Thomason   Philip Webb   Ernest Blythe   Pat Hagan   Edward Palmer   Pat Ryan

Philip Stewart   Daniel Brown   Jimmy Charters   Billy Davis   Hugh Futcher   Iris Fry   Victor Harrington

Ernest C. Jennings   Alf Mangan   Alan Meachum   Bob Ramsey   Ian Selby   John Smart   Ron Tarr

Rita Tobin   Joseph Tregonino   Mike Varey   Fred Woods   Council Member   Man 1   Man 2

Man 3   Man 4   Man 5   Man 6   Man 7   Man 8   Man 9

Man 10   Woman 1   Woman 2   Woman 3   Woman 4   Woman 5   Woman 6

Woman 7   Woman 8   Woman 9   Woman 10

169

Due to excessive rainy weather, the seaside town of Fircombe is facing a crisis. Councillor Sidney Fiddler comes up with the idea of having a beauty contest.

Frederick Bumble, the mayor, thinks the contest is a good idea, but feminist councillor Augusta Prodworthy is outraged. However, the contest gets the green light.

Sidney contacts publicist Peter Potter to help with the organization. Connie Philpotts, Sid's girlfriend, runs a local hotel and her residents-including the eccentric Mrs. Dukes and the randy old Admiral-are soon descended upon by models.

The girls include diminutive biker Hope Springs and tall, buxom Dawn Brakes. A fight ensues after Hope thinks Dawn has stolen her bikini costume.

Kenneth Connor, Patricia Franklin, Billy Cornelius, David Lodge, June Whitfield

Film Poster

Patricia Franklin, June Whitfield

Peter Butterworth, Barbara Windsor

Valerie Leon, Bernard Bresslaw

Kenneth Connor, Marianne Stone

This makes better newspaper copy than bringing a donkey off the beach (which ruins the plush carpets). Augusta's son, press photographer Larry, is hired to document the donkey stunt.

Instead he photographs the catfight that has the Mayor losing his trousers. Mildred Bumble, the Mayor's wife, joins Augusta; they plot the downfall of the Miss Fircombe contest on the pier.

Peter Potter reluctantly becomes a man in a frock for another publicity gimmick for the television show *Women's Things*, presented by Cecil Gaybody.

Film Poster

Jimmy Logan, Barbara Windsor et al

Joan Sims, Sidney James

Kenneth Connor, Marianne Stone,
June Whitfield

Peter Butterworth, Angela Grant,
Sidney James

Lobby Card

Kenneth Connor, Patsy Rowlands

Augusta calls the police to investigate the male pageant contestant, but Peter's previously prim girlfriend, Paula, has a makeover and turns out to be very buxom and glamorous.

After the final contest is sabotaged with itching powder, water, and mud an angry mob chases Sidney, who makes his escape on a go-kart. Discovering that Connie has absconded with the money, Sid speeds off with Hope on her motorcycle.

Foreign Film Poster

Margaret Nolan, Valerie Leon, Barbara Windsor

Joan Sims, Joan Hickson

Sidney James, Jack Douglas

Sally Geeson, Jimmy Logan

Joan Sims, Sidney James

Lobby Card

CARRY ON DICK (1974)

DIRECTED BY Gerald Thomas

CAST

Sidney James...Big Dick Turpin/Reverend Flasher
Barbara Windsor..............................Harriet
Kenneth Williams...Captain Desmond Fancey
Hattie Jacques.................Martha Hoggett
Bernard Bresslaw............Sir Roger Daley
Joan Sims.......................Madame Desiree
Kenneth Connor.......................Constable
Peter Butterworth..............................Tom
Jack Douglas..................Sgt. Jock Strapp
Patsy Rowlands......................Mrs. Giles
Bill Maynard...............................Bodkin
Margaret Nolan.......................Mrs. Daley
John Clive......................Isaac the Tailor
David Lodge...............................Bullock
Marianne Stone...........................Maggie
Patrick Durkin............................William
Sam Kelly...............................Coachman
George Moon..........................Mr. Giles
Michael Nightingale.....Squire Trelawney
Brian Osborne.........................Browning
Anthony Bailey..............................Rider
Brian Coburn..........Scottish Highwayman
Max Faulkner......................Highwayman
Joy Harrington...............................Lady
James Payne.............Bow Street Runner
Rita Tobin...............................Old Lady
Gerry Wain............................Horsemaster

Sidney James   Barbara Windsor   Kenneth Williams

Hattie Jacques   Bernard Bresslaw   Joan Sims

Kenneth Connor   Peter Butterworth   Jack Douglas

Patsy Rowlands   Bill Maynard   Margaret Nolan

John Clive   David Lodge   Marianne Stone

173

Tim Turner.....................................Narrator
Billy Cornelius, Larry Taylor.........Toughs
Tony Castleton, Mike Stevens...Policemen
George Hilsdon, Eric Kent, Tom Marshall
....Churchgoers
Jeremy Connor, Nosher Powell, Michael
Stainton..Footpads
Laraine Humphrys, Linda Hooks, Penny
Irving, Eva Reuber-Staier.......Entertainers
Harry Fielder, Nick Hobbs, Stephen
Kemble, Lou Morgan, Gerald Paris, Bob
Ramsey.........................Tavern Customers

Patrick Durkin   Sam Kelly   George Moon

Michael Nightingale   Brian Osborne   Anthony Bailey

Brian Coburn   Max Faulkner   Joy Harrington

James Payne   Rita Tobin   Billy Cornelius   Larry Taylor   Tony Castleton   Mike Stevens   George Hilsdon

Eric Kent   Jeremy Connor   Nosher Powell   Laraine Humphrys   Linda Hooks   Penny Irving   Eva Reuber-Staier

Harry Fielder   Lou Morgan   Gerald Paris   Bob Ramsey   Man 1   Man 2   Man 3

Man 4   Man 5   Man 6   Man 7   Woman 1   Woman 2   Woman 3

174

91 minutes

Foreign Film Poster

In 1750 England, the Bow Street Runners, the first professional police force, is set up to deal with rampant crime, especially highway robbery. The crime spree has produced much anxiety.

The new force comes under the command of Sir Roger Daley, and seconded by Captain Desmond Fancey and Sergeant Jock Strapp. The Runners are apparently successful in wiping out crime and lawlessness.

They employ numerous tricks and traps for the criminals. So far they have been unable to catch the notorious Richard "Big Dick" Turpin, a highwayman.

Peter Butterworth, Kenneth Connor

Hattie Jacques as Martha Hoggett

Joan Sims, Sidney James

Big Dick also had the nerve to rob Sir Roger and his wife of their money and clothing. After this humiliation, Turpin becomes the Bow Street Runners' most wanted man.

However, Turpin manages to outsmart Sergeant Strapp, sending him away in the coach of French showwoman Madame Desiree, and her daughters.

Captain Fancey is assigned to go undercover and catch the infamous Dick Turpin. The Bow Street Runners almost succeed in apprehending Turpin and his two partners in crime, Harriet and Tom.

In the village of Upper Dencher, near to where the majority of Turpin's hold-ups are carried out, Fancey and Strapp meet mild-mannered Reverend Flasher, who is in fact Turpin in disguise.

Hattie Jacques eavesdropping

Barbara Windsor, Sidney James

Lobby Card

Film Poster

Fancey and Strapp mistakenly take Turpin into their confidence, meeting at the low-life Old Cock Inn, a notorious hang-out for criminals and sleazy types.

After discovering Big Dick has a birthmark on his buttocks, Strapp and Fancey send a message to Sir Roger about the birthmark, and are accosted by Harriet in disguise who tells them where to find Turpin.

Jack Douglas, Bernard Bresslaw,
Kenneth Williams, Kenneth Connor

Kenneth Williams, Bernard Bresslaw

Barbara Windsor, Hattie Jacques,
Sidney James

Lobby Card

Kenneth Williams, Jack Douglas

Lobby Card

177

Naturally, things go wrong for Fancey and Strapp; they are imprisoned by Turpin and his mate, and Sir Roger is yet again robbed on his way to see the prisoners.

Just when it seems Turpin will finally be apprehended, the Reverend Flasher gives a long sermon before outwitting his would-be captors once more, and makes a quick getaway across the border.

Lobby Card

Bernard Bresslaw, Margaret Nolan

Bernard Bresslaw, Jack Douglas

Hattie Jacques, Sidney James

George Moon, Patsy Rowlands

Hattie Jacques, Peter Butterworth

CARRY ON BEHIND (1975)

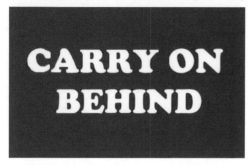

DIRECTED BY Gerald Thomas

CAST

Elke Sommer......Professor Anna Vooshka
Kenneth Williams....Professor Roland Crump
Bernard Bresslaw..............Arthur Upmore
Kenneth Connor.....................Major Leep
Jack Douglas.........................Ernie Bragg
Joan Sims.........................Daphne Barnes
Windsor Davies.................Fred Ramsden
Peter Butterworth...............Henry Barnes
Liz Fraser.......................Sylvia Ramsden
Patsy Rowlands.................Linda Upmore
Ian Lavender...........................Joe Baxter
Adrienne Posta...................Norma Baxter
Patricia Franklin.....................Vera Bragg
Donald Hewlett.........................The Dean
Carol Hawkins..............................Sandra
Sherrie Hewson...............................Carol
David Lodge..............................Landlord
Marianne Stone....................Mrs. Rowan
George Layton.............................Doctor
Brian Osborne..................................Bob
Larry Dann.....................................Clive
Georgina Moon...............................Sally
Diana Darvey............................Maureen
Jenny Cox..................................Veronica
Larry Martyn..........................Electrician
Linda Hooks.................................Nurse
Kenneth Waller............................Barman

Elke Sommer   Kenneth Williams   Bernard Bresslaw

Kenneth Connor   Jack Douglas   Joan Sims

Windsor Davies   Peter Butterworth   Liz Fraser

Patsy Rowlands   Ian Lavender   Adrienne Posta

Patricia Franklin   Donald Hewlett   Carol Hawkins

179

Billy Cornelius.................Man With Salad
Melita Manger.............Woman With Salad
Helli Louise.....................................Nudist
Jeremy Connor....Student With Ice Cream
Alexandra Dane...Lady in Low-Cut Dress
Johnny Briggs.............................Plasterer
Brenda Cowling.................................Wife
Ray Edwards..................Man With Water
Lucy Griffiths....................Lady With Hat
Sidney Johnson.............Bespectacled Man
Sam Kelly.............................Projectionist
Stanley McGeagh........Short-Sighted Man
Drina Pavlovic......................Courting Girl
James Payne....................Man in Caravan
Gerald Thomas...........Mynah Bird (voice)
Jerry Baker, Hugh Futcher, Alan Mea-
chum...Painters
Roderick Smith, Matthew Solon, Caroline
Whitaker..Students
Derek Chafer, George Hilsdon, Steve
Ismay, Kevin O'Shea, Peter Roy, Reg
Thomason......................Men in Audience

Sherrie Hewson   David Lodge   Marianne Stone

George Layton   Brian Osborne   Larry Dann

Georgina Moon   Diana Darvey   Jenny Cox

Larry Martyn   Linda Hooks   Kenneth Waller

Billy Cornelius   Melita Manger   Helli Louise

Jeremy Connor   Alexandra Dane   Johnny Briggs   Brenda Cowling   Lucy Griffiths   Sidney Johnson   Sam Kelly

Stanley McGeagh   James Payne   Gerald Thomas   Hugh Futcher   Alan Meachum   Derek Chafer   George Hilsdon

Peter Roy	Reg Thomason	Man 1	Man 2	Man 3	Man 4	Man 5
Man 6	Mynah Bird	Woman 1	Woman 2	Woman 3	Woman 4	Woman 5

90 minutes

Butcher Fred Ramsden and his slow-witted electrician friend Ernie Bragg happily head off for a holiday trip at the Riverside Caravan Site, while their respective wives Sylvia and Vera look forward to their trip to a health farm.

Once at the caravan site of Major Leep, Fred starts making eyes at two young female campers, Carol and Sandra. However, as Ernie talks in his sleep and any infidelities are likely to be picked up in bed after their holiday by Mrs. Bragg, Fred is despondent.

Professor Roland Crump teams with Roman expert Anna Vrooshka in an archaeological dig at the site. Arthur Upmore and his wife Linda are saddled with her mother Daphne and her vulgar mynah bird.

Elke Sommer, Kenneth Williams

Windsor Davies, Liz Fraser

Arthur is caught in a compromising position with attractive blonde Norma Baxter whose husband Joe is lumbered with their giant Irish wolfhound.

After a few drinks with the amused pub landlord, Fred and Ernie discover that the caravan site is riddled with excavation holes. Daphne is perturbed by the discovery that her estranged husband Henry Barnes lives a downtrodden life as the camp's odd-job man, despite having won the pools.

Foreign Film Poster

The beautiful Elke Sommer

Elke Sommer, Kenneth Williams

Elke Sommer, Kenneth Connor

Film Poster

Lobby Card

Windsor Davies, Carol Hawkins

Lobby Card

Elke Sommer, Kenneth Williams,
Peter Butterworth

Elke Sommer, Kenneth Williams

Foreign Film Poster

Major Leep is determined to give the place a boost and arranges an evening cabaret for the caravan owners, but a mix-up over the phone secures a stripper, Veronica, rather than the singer he wanted.

Bernard Bresslaw, Elke Sommer

Windsor Davies, Elke Sommer, Larry
Martyn

Elke Sommer as Anna Vooshka

Sherrie Hewson, Carol Hawkins

Linda Hooks, George Layton

Adrienne Posta, Ian Lavender

Windsor Davies, Larry Martyn

Carol and Sandra having hooked up
with archaeology students Bob and
Clive, Fred and Ernie pick up Maureen and Sally, two beautiful young
women from the village.

Some wet paint, some glue, heavy
rain that causes the tunnels of the
dig to collapse, and the arrival of
their wives soon bring their planned
night of passion to a halt.

CARRY ON ENGLAND (1976)

DIRECTED BY Gerald Thomas

CAST

Kenneth Connor.............Captain S. Melly
Windsor Davies......Sgt. Major Tiger Bloomer
Judy Geeson...........Sergeant Tilly Willing
Patrick Mower.............Sergeant Len Able
Jack Douglas...............Bombardier Ready
Joan Sims......Pvt. Jennifer Ffoukes-Sharp
Melvyn Hayes.............Gunner Shorthouse
Peter Butterworth.............Major Carstairs
Peter Jones..................................Brigadier
Diane Langton..................Pvt. Alice Easy
Julian Holloway................Major Butcher
David Lodge........................Captain Bull
Larry Dann..........................Gunner Shaw
Brian Osborne....................Gunner Owen
Johnny Briggs...................Melly's Driver
Patricia Franklin................Corporal Cook
Linda Hooks.....................................Nurse
Vivienne Johnson.............................Freda
Jeremy Connor...............Gunner Hiscocks
Richard Olley....................Gunner Parker
Peter Banks.....................Gunner Thomas
Richard Bartlett...................Gunner Drury
Billy J. Mitchell.................Gunner Childs
Peter Quince.....................Gunner Sharpe
Peter Toothill........................Gunner Gale
Trisha Newby............Bombardier Murray
Paul Humpoletz.................Gunner Lewis

Kenneth Connor

Windsor Davies

Judy Geeson

Patrick Mower

Jack Douglas

Joan Sims

Melvyn Hayes

Peter Butterworth

Peter Jones

Diane Langton

Julian Holloway

David Lodge

Larry Dann

Brian Osborne

Johnny Briggs

Philip Barnes.............................Gunner
John Carlin, Michael Nightingale.......Officers
Louise Burton, Jeannie Collings, Barbara
Lampshire, Linda Regan, Barbara Rosenblat..
....A.T.S. Privates

Patricia Franklin   Linda Hooks   Vivienne Johnson

Jeremy Connor   Richard Olley   Peter Banks

Richard Bartlett   Billy J. Mitchell   Peter Quince   Peter Toothill   Trisha Newby   John Carlin   Michael Nightingale

Louise Burton   Jeannie Collings   Barbara Lampshire   Linda Regan   Barbara Rosenblat   Girl   Soldier

89 minutes

During the Second World War, circa 1940, Captain S. Melly is put in charge of an experimental mixed-battery. It's a pleasure for Captain Bull to greet his relief.

Melly however is not prepared for the ball-squeezing Sergeant Major Tiger Bloomer and the randy antics of Bombardier Ready, Sergeant Tilly Willing, and Sergeant Len Able.

Patricia Franklin as Corporal Cook

186

Melly arrives to find a guard wearing lipstick, and female underwear in full view on clothes lines. Perpetually feigning illness or hiding in their underground snoggery, the troops are happily getting to grips with each other rather than the enemy.

Melly's attempts to impose discipline make him unpopular, and the target of a series of rather nasty practical jokes, such as falling repeatedly in cow dung, having his uniform fall to pieces during a march, and his soap changed so that he turns blue when he next tries to shower.

Peter Butterworth, Peter Jones

Kenneth Connor, Windsor Davies

Kenneth Connor, Patrick Mower

Corporal with Kenneth Connor

Patrick Mower, Judy Geeson

Patrick Mower, Judy Geeson

Most prominent of the females is Private Alice Easy, who tries to charm her new commanding officer but only succeeds in propelling her top button into his system!

Private Jennifer Ffoukes-Sharpe pines for Tiger while everybody-including little Gunner Shorthouse-gets a piece of the action. Even after a tip-off to the medical officer, Major Butcher, segregation and rigorous training, the unit is still a mess.

Film Poster

Patrick Mower, Linda Hooks

Kenneth Connor, Melvyn Hayes

Kenneth Connor, Windsor Davies

Windsor Davies, Joan Sims

Kenneth Connor with bandaged fingers

Windsor Davies-no nonsense

Patrick Mower, Judy Geeson

Kenneth Connor, Windsor Davies

However, an inspection by the cowardly Brigadier and Major Carstairs is interrupted by an airborne attack and Melly's troops finally prove they are real British bulldogs.

Reviewers for the most part were critical of this film, pointing out weaknesses in nearly every aspect or performance of it. It was a commercial and critical failure, and seemed to put a nail in the coffin of the Carry On films.

Lobby Card

Patrick Mower, Peter Butterworth

Lobby Card

Joan Sims, Judy Geeson

THAT'S CARRY ON (1977)

DIRECTED BY Gerald Thomas

CAST

Kenneth Williams...........................Himself
Barbara Windsor............................Herself
Eric Barker, Bernard Bresslaw, Peter But-
terworth, Esma Cannon, Cyril Chamber-
lain, Tom Clegg, John Clive, Kenneth
Connor, Kenneth Cope, Billy Cornelius,
Bernard Cribbins, Jim Dale, Ed De-
vereaux, Angela Douglas, Jack Doug-
las, Shirley Eaton, Peter Gilmore, Fred
Griffiths, Anita Harris, Charles Hawtrey,
Percy Herbert, Joan Hickson, Julian Hol-
loway, Frankie Howerd, Hattie Jacques,
Sidney James, Gertan Klauber, Dilys
Laye, Valerie Leon, Harry Locke, Ter-
ence Longdon, Victor Maddern, Margaret
Nolan, Richard O'Callaghan, Julian Or-
chard, Bill Owen, Leslie Phillips, Jacki
Piper, Patsy Rowlands, Terry Scott, Val-
erie Shute, Joan Sims, Marianne Stone,
Larry Taylor, June Whitfield....................
....Multiple Roles

AND:

Amanda Barrie...........................Cleopatra
Susan Beaumont.................Frances James
John Bluthal...........................Royal Taylor

Kenneth Williams   Barbara Windsor   Eric Barker

Bernard Bresslaw   Peter Butterworth   Esma Cannon

Cyril Chamberlain   Tom Clegg   John Clive

Kenneth Connor   Kenneth Cope   Billy Cornelius

Bernard Cribbins   Jim Dale   Ed Devereaux

Sydney Bromley...................Sam Houston
Ray Brooks.....................................Georgio
Simon Cain..Short
Gerald Campion...............Andy Calloway
Roy Castle..........................Captain Keene
Norman Chappell.........................Allbright

Angela Douglas   Jack Douglas   Shirley Eaton

Peggy Ann Clifford.............Willa Claudia
Harry H. Corbett....Det. Sgt. Sidney Bung
David Davenport...............................Bilius
Windsor Davies..................Fred Ramsden
Sally Douglas.....................Dusky Maiden

Peter Gilmore   Fred Griffiths   Anita Harris

Fenella Fielding....................Valerie Watt
Frank Forsyth.............................Specialist
Lucy Griffiths..............................Old Lady
William Hartnell.......Sergeant Grimshawe
Imogen Hassall.....................Jenny Grubb

Charles Hawtrey   Percy Herbert   Joan Hickson

Wilfrid Hyde-White......................Colonel
Penny Irving...Lizzy
June Jago............................Sister Hoggett
Rosalind Knight..............Felicity Wheeler
Ann Lancaster.....................Miss Armitage

Julian Holloway   Frankie Howerd   Hattie Jacques

Jimmy Logan........................Bert Conway
Kenny Lynch....................Bus Conductor
Elspeth March......................Lady Binder
Betty Marsden.........................Mata Hari
Freddie Mills..........................Jewel Thief

Sidney James   Gertan Klauber   Dilys Laye

Juliet Mills..Sally
Warren Mitchell.........................Spencius
Bob Monkhouse...................Charlie Sage
Michael Nightingale..........Cinema Patron
Brian Oulton...................................Brutus

Valerie Leon   Harry Locke   Terence Longdon

Lance Percival...................Wilfred Haines
Ted Ray........................William Wakefield
Anthony Sagar...................Bus Conductor
Phil Silvers.....................Sergeant Nocker
Madeline Smith.......................Mrs. Pullitt

Victor Maddern   Margaret Nolan   Richard O'Callaghan

Elke Sommer......Professor Anna Vooshka
Susan Stephen........Nurse Georgie Axwell
Julie Stevens.....................................Gloria

Jimmy Thompson....................Sam Turner
Valerie Van Ost......................Nurse Parkin
Wanda Ventham....................Pretty Bidder

Julian Orchard   Bill Owen   Leslie Phillips

Jacki Piper   Patsy Rowlands   Terry Scott   Valerie Shute   Joan Sims   Marianne Stone   Larry Taylor

June Whitfield   Amanda Barrie   Susan Beaumont   John Bluthal   Sydney Bromley   Ray Brooks   Simon Cain

Gerald Campion   Roy Castle   Norman Chappell   Peggy Ann Clifford   Harry H. Corbett   David Davenport   Windsor Davies

Sally Douglas   Fenella Fielding   Frank Forsyth   Lucy Griffiths   William Hartnell   Imogen Hassall   Wilfrid Hyde-White

Penny Irving   June Jago   Rosalind Knight   Ann Lancaster   Jimmy Logan   Kenny Lynch   Elspeth March

Betty Marsden   Freddie Mills   Juliet Mills   Warren Mitchell   Bob Monkhouse   Michael Nightingale   Brian Oulton

Lance Percival   Ted Ray   Anthony Sagar   Phil Silvers   Madeline Smith   Elke Sommer   Susan Stephen

Julie Stevens   Jimmy Thompson   Valerie Van Ost   Wanda Ventham   Derek Francis

That's Carry On is a movie with Kenneth Williams and Barbara Windsor introducing clips from all the Carry On films. The two regulars converse at the Rank Film building to host the film, with their own running gags involving Barbara's "assets" and Kenneth's desperate need of a toilet.

At Pinewood Studious, Kenneth Williams and Barbara Windsor are imprisoned in a projection room and search through film cans that contain the Carry On series.

Sidney James

Sidney James, Bernard Bresslaw, Joan Sims

Kenneth Williams, Jack Douglas

Angela Douglas with pistols

Film Poster

Film Poster

Barbara Windsor, Sidney James

Peter Butterworth with ball

Kenneth is delighted with the food basket and champagne, while Barbara loads the vintage clips. As the films play, Kenneth feels the need to use the toilet, while Barbara is determined to look at all the films.

Kenneth almost can't take any more when he sees scenes of speedy urination from *Carry On at Your Convenience*, but stick around to watch himself in another clip.

Finally, he can't hold it any longer, and when Barbara leaves the projection room and locks her co-star in, he decides to relieve himself against the door.

The idea for the film was inspired by M-G-Ms *That's Entertainment*. *That's Carry On* was released in 1977 as a supporting feature to *The Golden Rendezvous*, starring Richard Harris.

Fenella Fielding, Kenneth Williams

Barbara Windsor, Kenneth Williams

Kenneth Williams, Barbara Windsor

Sidney James, Percy Herbert, Joan Sims

Barbara Windsor and Kenneth Williams

One reviewer said *"That's Carry On* is an okay compilation of the highlights from Britain's legendary Carry On series of theatrical farces. Series veterans Kenneth Williams and Barbara Windsor act as hosts, mugging their way through so-so material."

Amanda Barrie, Sidney James

Film Poster

Barbara Windsor, Kenneth Williams

Elke Sommer, Kenneth Connor

This is not a documentary but a compilation of some of the best gags from the long running Carry On movie series. It takes you through what was then 28 films in the series. This is a fairly good way to get an idea of what the movies were, the slapstick, the double entendres, the silliness and sometimes crudeness.

Harry H. Corbett

Sidney James, Joan Sims

Barbara Windsor with film cans

CARRY ON EMMANNUELLE (1978)

DIRECTED BY Gerald Thomas

CAST

Kenneth Williams................Emile Prevert
Kenneth Connor..........................Leyland
Joan Sims................................Mrs. Dangle
Jack Douglas.....................................Lyons
Peter Butterworth.....................Richmond
Suzanne Danielle....Emmannuelle Prevert
Beryl Reid..........................Mrs. Valentine
Larry Dann.................Theodore Valentine
Henry McGee......................Harold Hump
Victor Maddern..........Man in Launderette
Guy Ward..Dandy
Dino Shafeek.............Immigration Officer
Eric Barker.....................Ancient General
Joan Benham.......................Cynical Lady
James Fagan.................Concorde Steward
Malcolm Johns...............................Sentry
Albert Moses..................................Doctor
Robert Dorning.................Prime Minister
Steve Plytas.....................Arabian Official
Michael Nightingale......Police Commissioner
Claire Davenport................Blonde in Pub
Bruce Boa......................U.S. Ambassador
Llewellyn Rees............Lord Chief Justice
Jack Lynn..................Admiral of the Fleet
Norman Mitchell..........Drunken Husband
Tricia Newby.......................Surgery Nurse
Deborah Brayshaw............Buxom Blonde

Kenneth Williams   Kenneth Connor   Joan Sims

Jack Douglas   Peter Butterworth   Suzanne Danielle

Beryl Reid   Larry Dann   Henry McGee

Victor Maddern   Guy Ward   Dino Shafeek

Eric Barker   Joan Benham   James Fagan

John Carlin..........................French Parson
Louise Burton..........................Girl at Zoo
Gertan Klauber..................German Soldier
Suzanna East.....................................Colette
Howard Nelson.....................Harry Hernia
Bruce Wyllie....................Football Referee
Marianne Maskell.............Maternity Nurse
Philip Clifton..................Injured Footballer
Stanley McGeagh.....Fleet Street Journalist
Corbett Woodall................ITN Newscaster
Nick White....................Booked Footballer
Tim Brinton.................B.B.C. Newscaster
Walter Henry.....................Customs Officer
Ken Lawrie......................................Referee
Aileen Lewis..........................Dinner Guest
Reuben Martin..................................Gorilla
Edwin Fowles, James Payne.....Pub Customers
Jack Armstrong, Ishaq Bux, John Clifford,
John More.......................Plane Passengers
John Hallet, Lloyd McGuire, Nigel Miles-
Thomas, Charles Nicklin, Jeff Pirie............
....Footballers
Tony Clarkin, Bill Hutchinson, Maureen
Nelson, Jane Norman, Neville Ware..........
....Reporters
Shirley English, Ronald Nunnery, Gerald
Paris, Laurie Rose, Pat Ryan...Football Fans

Malcolm Johns   Albert Moses   Robert Dorning

Steve Plytas   Michael Nightingale   Claire Davenport

Bruce Boa   Llewellyn Rees   Jack Lynn

Norman Mitchell   Tricia Newby   Deborah Brayshaw

John Carlin   Louise Burton   Gertan Klauber

Howard Nelson   Bruce Wyllie   Marianne Maskell

Philip Clifton   Stanley McGeagh   Corbett Woodall   Nick White   Tim Brinton   Walter Henry   Ken Lawrie

200

Aileen Lewis	Reuben Martin	Edwin Fowles	Jack Armstrong	Ishaq Bux	John More	John Hallet
Bill Hutchinson	Maureen Nelson	Jane Norman	Neville Ware	Shirley English	Ronald Nunnery	Gerald Paris

Laurie Rose   Pat Ryan

The beautiful and sex-starved Emmannuelle Prevert just cannot inflame her husband's attention. In frustration she seduces a string of VIPs, including the Prime Minister and the American Ambassador.

Emmannuelle relieves the boredom of a flight on a concorde by seducing timid Theodore Valentine. She returns home to London to surprise her husband, the French ambassador, Émile Prevert, but first surprises the butler, Lyons.

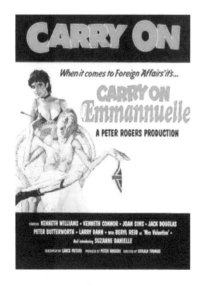

Film Poster

The Scales of Justice

He removes her coat, only to find that she has left her dress on the aircraft. The chauffeur, Leyland, housekeeper, Mrs Dangle, and aged boot-boy, Richmond, sense troubled times ahead.

Émile is dedicated to his body-building, leaving a sexually frustrated Emmannuelle to find pleasure with everyone from the Lord Chief Justice to chat show host, Harold Hump.

Reporters on the film

CARRY ON *Emmannuelle*

Movie Still

Jack Douglas, Kenneth Connor

CARRY ON *Emmannuelle*

Movie Still

Underwater scene

Kenneth Williams, Suzanne Danielle

Kenneth Williams, Suzanne Danielle,
Jack Douglas

Kenneth Connor, Claire Davenport

A smiling Beryl Reid

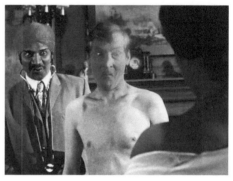

Albert Moses, Kenneth Williams

Howard Nelson, Suzanne Danielle

Suzanne Danielle, Jack Douglas,
Kenneth Williams

Theodore is spurned by Emmannu-elle, who has genuinely forgotten their airborne encounter, and, de-spite reassurances from his mother, exacts revenge by revealing Em-mannuelle's antics to the press. Af-ter a scandal ensues, she discovers that she is pregnant and decides to settle down to a faithful marriage with Émile.

One reviewer stated *"Carry On Emmannuelle* is easily the worst film of the series. It also did even worse at the box office than *Carry On England*. The two failures were too much for the series to withstand, and it ended."

Another said *"Carry on Emmannuelle* is regarded as the worst of the "Carry On" movies and it really is. Everything which was good and entertaining about the "Carry On" movies is missing, replaced by unintelligent smut."

Film Poster

Suzanne Danielle and guard

Peter Butterworth lends an ear

Joan Sims, Jack Douglas, Kenneth Connor, Peter Butterworth

Joan Benham being attentive

Bad time for a phone call

CARRY ON COLUMBUS (1992)

DIRECTED BY Gerald Thomas

CAST

Jim Dale................Christopher Columbus
Bernard Cribbins........Mordecai Mendoza
Maureen Lipman.......Countess Esmeralda
Peter Richardson..............Bart Columbus
Alexei Sayle....................................Achmed
Leslie Phillips..................King Ferdinand
June Whitfield...................Queen Isabella
Rik Mayall.....................................Sultan
Charles Fleischer.........................Pontiac
Larry Miller...........................The Chief
Nigel Planer............................The Wazir
Julian Clary....................Don Juan Diego
Sara Crowe....................................Fatima
Richard Wilson...............Don Juan Felipe
James Faulkner.....................Torquemada
Burt Kwouk.....................................Wang
Holly Aird.......................................Maria
Keith Allen....................Pepe the Poisoner
Martin Clunes...............................Martin
Jack Douglas.......Marco the Cereal Killer
Allan Corduner....................................Sam
Peter Gordeno.......................The Shaman
Don Henderson........................The Bosun
Rebecca Lacey...........................Chiquita
Chris Langham..............................Hubba
Danny Peacock.................Tonto the Torch
Jon Pertwee..............Duke of Costa Brava

Jim Dale

Bernard Cribbins

Maureen Lipman

Peter Richardson

Alexei Sayle

Leslie Phillips

June Whitfield

Rik Mayall

Charles Fleischer

Larry Miller

Nigel Planer

Julian Clary

Sara Crowe

Richard Wilson

James Faulkner

Tony Slattery.............Baba the Messenger
Andrew Bailey.............................Genghis
Philip Herbert..................................Ginger
David Boyce...............Customer With Ear
Sara Stockbridge..............Nina the Model
Su Douglas.....................Countess Joanna
John Antrobus.........................Manservant
Lynda Baron..Meg
Nejdet Salih....................................Fayid
Mark Arden..Mark
Silvestre Tobias..........................Abdullah
Harold Berens...............Cecil the Torturer
Peter Gilmore....Governor of the Canaries
Marc Sinden........................Captain Perez
Reed Martin...........................Poca Hontas
Prudence Solomon..........................Ha Ha
Peter Grant................................Cardinal
Peter Pedrero........................Native Guard
Lorraine Sass.........Girl in Spanish Court
Joanna Stride...................Sultan's Servant
Toby Dale, Duncan Duff, Dave Freeman,
Michael Hobbs, Don MacLean, James
Pertwee, Jonathan Tafler..........Inquisitors

Burt Kwouk   Holly Aird   Keith Allen

Martin Clunes   Jack Douglas   Allan Corduner

Peter Gordeno   Don Henderson   Rebecca Lacey

Chris Langham   Danny Peacock   Jon Pertwee

Tony Slattery   Andrew Bailey   Philip Herbert

David Boyce   Sara Stockbridge   Su Douglas   John Antrobus   Lynda Baron   Nejdet Salih   Mark Arden

Silvestre Tobias   Harold Berens   Peter Gilmore   Marc Sinden   Reed Martin   Prudence Solomon   Lorraine Sass

Don MacLean Man 1 Man 2 Man 3 Man 4 Woman 1 Woman 2

Woman 3 Woman 4

91 minutes

Christopher Columbus believes he can find an alternative route to the far East and persuades the King and Queen of Spain to finance his expedition.

Instead of experienced sailors, there are only convicts whose last and only meeting with H2O was their prison diet of bread and water. And Columbus doesn't have his own map.

Film Poster

Film Poster

Jim Dale and Sara Crowe

The Sultan of Turkey, who makes a great deal of money through taxing the merchants who have to pass through his country on the current route, sends his best spy, Fatima, to wreck the trip.

Reviewers primarily panned this film; however it did surprisingly better at the box office. One reviewer said " Perhaps the one imaginative aspect of this film is the portrayal of American Indians as street-smart wisecrackers who remark to themselves in broad New York accents about how primitive are the gold-grubbing Europeans who have landed on their shores.

Jim Dale licking his fingers

Black attired monks

Film Poster Foreign Film Poster

Richard Wilson, Maureen Lipman

Leslie Phillips, June Whitfield

But this comes only after an hour of tired costume drama that revels only in cleavage and homophobia. Moreover, the portrayal is inconsistent, as the indigenous have to be kitted out with an obligatory shaman, as well as propositions to bed the visiting countess.

They do have the last laugh, as they send Columbus and crew packing with what is literally fool's gold. But as with the rest of the film, it's not really much of a laugh in the end.

Alexei Sayle, Peter Richardson, Jim Dale, Sara Crowe, Bernard Cribbins

Foreign Film Poster

Jim Dale, Julian Clary

Jim Dale, Bernard Cribbins

Women of the royal court

Jim Dale as Christopher Columbus

Maureen Lipman, Rik Mayall

209

Carry on Columbus ends up a misguided attempt to try and bring "Carry On" back. Despite the best attempts of Jim Dale it doesn't work because sadly the "Carry On" movies ended up about the likes of Sidney James, Joan Sims and Kenneth Williams, and without them it just doesn't work."

Bernard Cribbins, Jim Dale

Jim Dale on ship

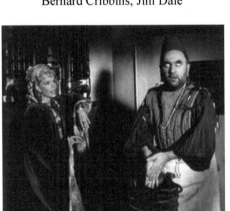

Sara Crowe, Alexei Sayle

Having a few drinks

Film Poster